This standard format verbal reasoning book contains 850 questio
detachable answer sheets. Each test can be completed in under one hour.
It is a compilation of all the work in Learning Together's *Verbal Reasoning Books 3 & 4*.

More Verbal Reasoning Tests is book 2 in a set of 2 and the preceding book is called
Verbal Reasoning Tests.

The book is an excellent aid in preparing children for their 11+ or 12+ examinations.
It can also be used in preparing children for grammar school, independent and private
school selection tests and contains work suitable for the CEM tests.
(These tests vary depending on the Local Education Authority or school. You should check
requirements with your Local Education Authority or school.)

The authors are experienced teachers and tutors who have developed and used these tests
extensively in the classroom over a number of years.

Working through these tests will provide children with experience of formal testing while
at the same time helping them to become more familiar with various types of verbal
reasoning question.

The Learning Together range of Verbal Reasoning books complements their range of
Non-Verbal Reasoning books and their *"How to do"* Non-Verbal and *Verbal Reasoning Step by
Step* books.

Stephen McConkey MA(Ed) BEd(Hons)
Tom Maltman BA

Published 2015
ISBN 978-1-873385-37-1

LEARNING TOGETHER

ADVICE AND INSTRUCTIONS ON COMPLETING THESE TESTS

1. There are 85 questions in each test. Make sure you have not missed a page.

2. Start at question 1 and work your way to question 85.

3. If you are unable to complete a question leave it and go to the next one.

4. Do not think about the question you have just left as this wastes time.

5. If you change an answer make sure the change is clear.

6. Make sure you spell correctly.

7. You may do any rough work on the test paper or on another piece of paper.

8. Each test should take approximately 50 minutes.

9. When you have finished each test mark it with an adult.

10. An adult may be able to explain any questions you do not understand.

TEST 11

SCORE _____

Do not make illegal copies of this test.

1. Write down any letter which occurs once in REVERBERANT and twice in RESONANCE. (_____)

2. Write down any letter which occurs once in CONDENSATION and twice in EVAPORATION. (_____)

3. Which letter occurs in JOANNE but not in JOAN? (_____)

4. A number plus one third of six equals 10. What is the number? (_____)

Share 15 apples between Olivia and Jack so that for every ONE apple Olivia gets Jack gets TWO apples.

5. How many apples does Jack get? (_____)

6. How many apples does Olivia get? (_____)

7. How many less than Jack did Olivia get? (_____)

In the questions below TWO words must change places so that the sentences make sense. Underline the TWO words that must change places.

Look at this example: **The <u>wood</u> was made of <u>table</u>.**

8. The fan had broken its car belt.

9. When they climbed to the rain the top had stopped.

10. The ship sailed anchor and lifted away.

11. A page was note from the torn book.

12. What dinner we having for our are to-day?

The table below gives some information about the addition of numbers in the left hand column to numbers in the top row. Complete the table.

+	0.3	2.2	1.4
0.7	1.0	2.9	2.1
1.6	1.9		
1.2	1.5		

13, 14, (row with 1.6)

15, 16 (row with 1.2)

In the following questions write in the brackets one letter which will complete the word in front of the brackets AND the word after the brackets.

Look at this example: ROA (D) OOR.

17. BOTTO (____) OUSE.

18. FU   (____) AT.

19. VER   (____) ACHT.

20. CRIS   (____) RICE.

21. WRIN   (____) RAIN.

22. BEN   (____) EAR.

Complete the sequences by inserting the correct numbers or letters in the brackets.

A B C D E F G H I J K L M N O P Q R S T U V W X Y Z

23. A   D   F   I   (_____)

24. ZY   WV   SR   NM   (_____)

25. FGH   EFG   DEF   CDE   (_____)

26. WV   TU   SR   PQ   (_____)

27. 1.5   3.0   4.5   6.0   (_____)

28. 25   21   17   13   (_____)

29. 162   54   18   6   (_____)

30. 9.8   10.9   12   13.1   (_____)

In each line below a word from the left-hand group joins with one from the right-hand group to make a new word. The left-hand word always comes first. Underline the chosen words.

Look at this example:

CORN	**FARM**	TIME	OVER	FIELD	**YARD**
31. FOR	LONG	DAM	TELL	CAST	SAKE
32. BLISS	DEEP	DAM	TEAR	PEN	SELL
33. ROBE	JERK	TALK	ART	IN	LIKE
34. PASS	FEW	SAD	ABLE	ILL	DOCK
35. TAB	OVER	INN	LET	TUNE	LOW
36. TALE	ON	MAN	TILL	OR	TELL

In the sentences below there are 4 words missing. Choose the MOST SUITABLE words from the lists A to D to complete the sentences. Choose a word from list A for space A, a word from list B for space B and so on.

Underline the words you choose.

As the weather got more (A) we (B) together to try to keep (C). We hoped that soon the people would begin to (D) for us.

37A.	38B.	39C.	40D.
pleasant	cried	dry	pray
wet	walked	warm	hope
miserable	shivered	hungry	talk
deteriorate	laughed	awake	search
hot	huddled	asleep	cry

£43.97 was made up using the smallest number of notes and coins shown below. How many of each were used?

41.   £10 notes   (____)   42. 50p coins   (____)   43.   20p coins   (____)

44.   2p coins   (____)   45. 1p coins   (____)

Thermometers are drawn below. The arrows point to temperatures. Read the temperatures and enter them into the brackets below the thermometers.

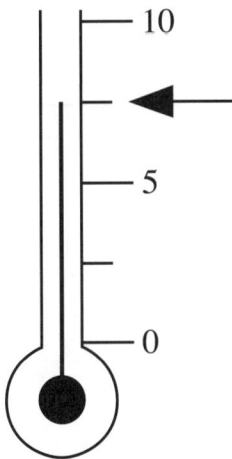

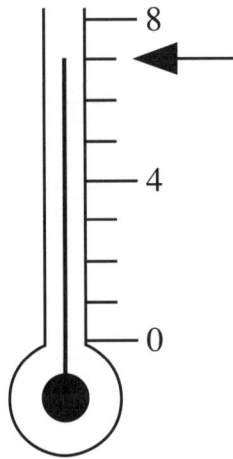

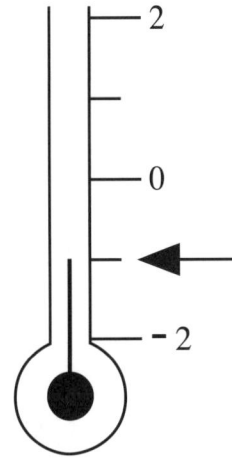

46. (_____)   47. (_____)   48. (_____)

Arrange the following words in alphabetical order.

enclose,　　　　　emery,　　　　　emend,　　　　　enamel,　　　　　emerge.

49.(＿＿＿＿＿) 50.(＿＿＿＿＿) 51.(＿＿＿＿＿) 52.(＿＿＿＿＿) 53.(＿＿＿＿＿)

First　　　　　　　　　　　　　　　　　　　　　　　　　　　　　**last**

Oldborough School has three lessons each afternoon. Each lesson, except the second lesson, lasts for the same length of time. There is a 5 minute gap between each lesson. Complete the table below, which shows the times at which lessons begin and end.

		Begins	**Ends**
54.	First Lesson	1.25 pm	
55.	Second Lesson		2.35 pm
56.	Third Lesson		3.15 pm

In the following questions a letter can be taken from the first word and put into the second word to form TWO new words. Write both NEW words.

Look at this example:　　　**THEN**　　　**TANK**　　　**(TEN)**　　　**(THANK)**

The H moves from THEN to TANK and makes the new words TEN and THANK.

57. LATHER　　　TICK　　　(＿＿＿＿＿)　　　(＿＿＿＿＿)

58. FIORD　　　BAT　　　(＿＿＿＿＿)　　　(＿＿＿＿＿)

59. RINSE　　　KIT　　　(＿＿＿＿＿)　　　(＿＿＿＿＿)

60. LANCE　　　HARM　　　(＿＿＿＿＿)　　　(＿＿＿＿＿)

61. THERM　　　GALLEY　　　(＿＿＿＿＿)　　　(＿＿＿＿＿)

62. MAIZE　　　NOSE　　　(＿＿＿＿＿)　　　(＿＿＿＿＿)

63. FIRST　　　COW　　　(＿＿＿＿＿)　　　(＿＿＿＿＿)

64. CAMPS　　　ARROW　　　(＿＿＿＿＿)　　　(＿＿＿＿＿)

TEST 11 PAGE 5

In each question below a man <u>ALWAYS STARTS by facing NORTH</u>.

Decide which directions he would be facing if he made the following turns -

65. He turned a quarter turn clockwise followed by a three-quarter turn anti-clockwise. (_____)

66. He made a three-quarter turn clockwise, followed by a half turn anti-clockwise and then a quarter turn clockwise. (_____)

67. He turned through 360 degrees. (_____)

A word of FOUR letters is hidden in each of the sentences below. The hidden words begin at the end of a word and finish at the start of the next word.

Write the hidden words in the brackets.

Look at this example:
Ti<u>me</u> <u>an</u>d tide wait for no man. The answer is MEAN.

68. She attached the bow to the parcel. (_____)

69. I hope they are allowed to go. (_____)

70. The large kangaroo munched the green grass. (_____)

71. This is something you must do especially as it is so important. (_____)

72. The climber found a hidden cave in the mountains. (_____)

73. The landscape altered as we drove across the country. (_____)

Five children A, B, C, D and E returned from holiday with sticks of rock, games and toys as presents. Only B and D didn't have sticks of rock.
B was the only person with just one present and it was a game.
Only A and E did not have games. 4 children had toys.

74. Who brought only games and toys home? (_____)

75. Who brought 3 presents home? (_____)

76. Which 2 children had the same presents? (_____)

77. Altogether how many presents were taken home? (_____)

In the following questions one word can be put in front of each of the given words to form a new word.

Write the correct words in the brackets.

Look at this example: shell   shore   side   bird   (SEA)

78. get   land   night   summer   (_____)

79. dog   fire   powder   boat   (_____)

80. cast   pour   stream   trodden   (_____)

81. look   coat   throw   haul   (_____)

In each of the following questions the numbers in the second column are formed from the numbers in the first column by using the same rule. Put the correct answer in the bracket for each question.

82. 6 ⟶ 12   83. 36 ⟶ 5   84. 5 ⟶ 12

7 ⟶ 14   25 ⟶ 4   6 ⟶ 14

8 ⟶ 16   81 ⟶ 8   10 ⟶ 22

9 ⟶ (___)   49 ⟶ (___)   17 ⟶ (___)

85. 18 ⟶ 8

14 ⟶ 6

12 ⟶ 5

6 ⟶ (___)

TEST 12

SCORE _____

1. Which letter, occurring more than once, occurs as often in GEOSYNCLINE as it does in GENTLEMEN?　(＿＿＿＿＿)

2. Which letter occurs once in HUNDREDWEIGHT, once in KILOGRAM but not in WEIGHING?　(＿＿＿＿＿)

3. Which letter occurs as often in LAWLESS as it does in LAW-MAKER but does not occur in JUDGE?　(＿＿＿＿＿)

4. Charles adds 9 to a third of a number and gets 27. What is half of that number?　(＿＿＿＿＿)

5. Chocolate bars cost 7p. more than lollipops. Two bars and one lollipop cost 53p. How much for one lollipop?　(＿＿＿＿＿)

In the questions below TWO words must change places so that the sentence makes sense. Underline the TWO words that must change places.

Look at this example:　　**The <u>wood</u> was made of <u>table</u>.**

6. The television turned the child on.

7. The man took the picture framed to be valued.

8. The sun soon dried and blistered in the paint.

9. A computer program pressed the wrong button and lost the operator.

10. His present told him to choose a mother and put it in the car.

The table below gives some information about the addition of numbers in the left hand column to those in the top row.
Complete the table correctly using only the numbers given.

28.75,　22.7,　5.1,　35.95,　2.5,　27.3

11. 12.	+		9.7	
13. 14.	17.6			20.1
15. 16.	26.25	31.35		

In each line below write in the brackets one letter which completes the word in front of and the word after the brackets.

Look at this example: **ROA (D) OOR**

Here D completes ROAD and begins DOOR.

17. FOREIG   (____)   EWT

18. CRA   (____)   NU

19. ELUD   (____)   LBOW

20. GEA   (____)   EIGN

21. SOCIA   (____)   IBEL

In each line below, the first word can be changed into the last word in three stages.
Only ONE letter can be replaced at a time and proper words must be made each time.

Look at this example: tide   (ride) (rode)   rope

22. hail   (_____)   (_____)   pull

23. pink   (_____)   (_____)   cane

24. fact   (_____)   (_____)   lake

25. kerb   (_____)   (_____)   head

26. chin   (_____)   (_____)   shop

In each line below underline TWO words, ONE from each side, which together make ONE correctly spelt word. The word on the left always comes first.

Look at this example:

<u>BLACK</u> ALL TOP 　　　AND <u>BIRD</u> BOY

27. DO　　　　NOT　　　IS　　　　　NOW　　SENT　　ICE

28. BAG　　　　BOOK　　KNOW　　　AGE　　LED　　　CASE

29. PAGE　　　GLOW　　FAR　　　　ANT　　BEE　　　ASS

30. PLOUGH　STIR　　HERE　　　RING　　UP　　　ON

31. BUD　　　　ADD　　　SUIT　　　ON　　　IN　　　OR

32. VICAR　　WEST　　STUN　　　AGE　　LAW　　ANT

In each of the following questions the letters of a word have been jumbled up. Using the clue unjumble the letters and write the correct word in the brackets.

33. EPNILCS　　　　　You can write with these.　　　　　(_____)

34. RACAULLTCO　　You can do sums on this.　　　　　(_____)

35. DALINS　　　　　A piece of land surrounded by water.　(_____)

36. DPCOKAD　　　A small field for horses.　　　　　　(_____)

37. ONPAWE　　　　Object used for offence or defence.　　(_____)

Write in the brackets a word that rhymes with the second word and has a similar meaning to the first word.

Look at this example:　　　SICK MILL (____ILL____)

38. ANSWER　　STY　　(_____)

39. LIFT　　　　HAZE　　(_____)

40. CROWD　　ROB　　(_____)

**In the paragraph below five words are missing. Choose the most
appropriate words from the lists below. One word from list A fills the
space at A, one word from list B fills the space at B and so on.
Underline the words you choose.**

The Hallowe'en fireworks (A) into the cold (B) night. The children (C) with
amazement as the rockets burst into a (D) of brilliant colours and lit up the (E) night
sky.

41. A	42. B	43. C	44. D	45. E
SLID	CHRISTMAS	GASPED	RIVER	BRIGHT
JUMPED	OCTOBER	SHOUTED	MIDDLE	WET
EXPLODED	FEBRUARY	HID	CASCADE	CLOUDY
FELL	EASTER	WHISPERED	STREAM	DAWN
HURRIED	JULY	SANG	PUDDLE	DARK

**In the following questions a letter can be taken from the first word and put into the second word
to form TWO new words. The order of the letters is not changed. Write both NEW words.**

Example:	**THINS**	**TOUT**	**(THIN)**	**(STOUT)**

46. TREAT   PINT   (_____)   (_____)

47. FIND   RUM   (_____)   (_____)

48. VOICE   WING   (_____)   (_____)

49. GNASH   LINE   (_____)   (_____)

50. BLACK   RUE   (_____)   (_____)

Complete the sequences by inserting the correct numbers in the brackets.

51. 23.37,   23.45,   23.53,   00.01   (_____)

52. 4.15,   3.25,   2.35,   1.45   (_____)

53. (34,43),   (41,35),   (48,27),   (55,19)   (_____,_____)

54. 2,   7,   14,   23,   34   (_____)

55. 1024,   256,   64,   16   (_____)

Using the numbers 8, 5, 6 and 4 ONCE ONLY in each question, fill in the spaces in any way that will make the statements correct.
Look at this example: (8 + 5 + 6 + 4)= 23

56. (___ X ___) - (___ X ___)   = 28

57. (___ + ___ + ___) X ___   = 76

58. (___ - ___) - (___ - ___)   = 1

59. (___ + ___) X (___ + ___)   = 130

60. (___ X ___) - (___ + ___)   = 11

In questions 61-66 the three words A, B and C are in alphabetical order.
The word at B is missing and you are given a dictionary definition instead.
Write the correct word in the space.

Look at this example: A) Flap
                          B) (__Flare__) Distress signal from a boat
                          C) Flash

61. A) ANVIL
     B) (_ _ _ _ _ _ _)   Uneasy with fear.
     C) ANY

62. A) PLACK
     B) (_ _ _ _ _ _)   A deadly epidemic.
     C) PLAICE

63. A) FOUND
     B) (_ _ _ _ _ _ _ _)   A jet of water.
     C) FOUR

64. A) HIPPODROME
     B) (_ _ _ _)   To engage for wages.
     C) HIRSEL

65. A) JABBER
     B) (_ _ _ _ _ _)   A wild, dog-like animal.
     C) JACKAROO

66. A) MOUSSE
     B (_ _ _ _ _)   Opening in the head of an animal.
     C) MOVE

In each question 67 - 70 the numbers in the second column are formed from the numbers in the first column by using a certain rule. A different rule is used in each question.
Put the correct answer opposite the arrow.

67. 5 ⟶ 26   68. 12 ⟶ 15

6 ⟶ 37   16 ⟶ 20

7 ⟶ 50   20 ⟶ 25

8 ⟶ (_____)   28 ⟶ (_____)

69. 1 ⟶ 0   70. 5 ⟶ 17

2 ⟶ 3   80 ⟶ 242

3 ⟶ 8   7 ⟶ 23

6 ⟶ (_____)   90 ⟶ (_____)

From the following shapes select the shape or shapes which satisfy the statements given. They may satisfy the statement on all or on some occasions. Answer the questions by placing the letter of the shape or shapes in the brackets.

A	B	C
PARALLELOGRAM	RECTANGLE	SQUARE

D	E
TRIANGLE	TRAPEZIUM

71. Diagonals are of equal length.   (_____)

72. Diagonals are at right angles.   (_____)

73. Three different sized sides.   (_____)

74. Internal angles total 180 degrees.   (_____)

In the following questions letters stand for numbers. Calculate the answer to each sum and write its LETTER in the bracket.

Look at this example:

A = 7   B = 2   C = 4   D = 1   E = 5   B + C + D =   (__A__)

75. If A = 5   B = 6   C = 7   D = 8   E = 9   then

A + D − B   =   (_____)

76. If A = 33   B = 22   C = 3   D = 23   E = 2   then

B × C ÷ E   =   (_____)

77. If A = 4   B = 6   C = 15   D = 5   E = 3   then

C ÷ E × A − D   =   (_____)

78. If A = 5   B = 4   C = 6   D = 8   E = 3   then

A × E − D − B   =   (_____)

79. If A = 12   B = 5   C = 11   D = 9   E = 10   then

E × E ÷ B − D   =   (_____)

80. If A = 5   B = 2   C = 10   D = 4   E = 7   then

C ÷ A + E − D   =   (_____)

At one time £1 was worth 16 Croatian Kuna.
(In each question below the exchange rate is the same)

81. How many Kuna was £3.00 worth?   (_____ Kuna)

82. How many Kuna was £6.25 worth?   (_____ Kuna)

83. How many Kuna was £13.75 worth?   (_____ Kuna)

84. A man bought a souvenir for 280 Kuna.
How much was that in British money?   (£_____)

85. At the end of his holiday the man changed his money back into British money
and received £10.25. How many Kuna did he have?   (_____ Kuna)

TEST 13

1. Which letter occurs twice in INTERDICT, once in INTERCHANGE and three times in INTERDIGITAL?   (_____)

2. Which letter occurs as often in PIERCINGLY as it does in WHISTLES, but does not occur in PIGEON?   (_____)

3. Which letter occurs twice as often in DOMINEERING as it does in DONATION?   (_____)

4. Three times a number plus 5 is 44. What is twice that number minus 7?   (_____)

5. Throughout the winter a horse eats ⅓ of its bales of hay and ignores 64 bales of hay. How many bales of hay did the horse eat?   (_____)

In the questions below TWO words must change places so that the sentence makes sense. Underline the TWO words that must change places.

Look at this example.   The <u>wood</u> was made of <u>table</u>.

6. The grate burned brightly in the fire.

7. The untidy papers were covered with rooms.

8. The flowers been withered because they had not had watered.

9. The puncture by the tyre was caused in a nail.

10. The postman arrived with of sackful a mail.

The table below gives some information about the addition of numbers in the left-hand column to those in the top row. Complete the table.

	+		5.02
11.			
12.	6.28	7.36	
13.		3.96	7.9
14. 15.			5.1

Test 13 Page 1

In each line below write in the brackets one letter which completes the word in front of and the word after the brackets.

Look at this example.   ROA (D) OOR

16.   ARTIS   (_____)   ITLE

17.   SING   (_____)   LEGANT

18.   STAM   (_____)   RISON

19.   STEA   (_____)   AUGH

20.   GROI   (_____)   OURISH

In the following questions a letter can be taken from the first word and put into the second word to form TWO new words. Write both NEW words.

Look at this example: THEN   TANK   (TEN)   (THANK)
The H moves from THEN to TANK and makes the new words TEN and THANK.

21.   BRAKE   BASS   (_____)   (_____)

22.   GRANGE   RUB   (_____)   (_____)

23.   LIED   MOST   (_____)   (_____)

24.   POUND   HOSING   (_____)   (_____)

25.   CLONE   PANE   (_____)   (_____)

In each line below underline TWO words, ONE from each side, which together make ONE correctly spelt word. The word on the left always comes first.

Look at this example:

BLACK	ALL	TOP	AND	**BIRD**	BOY
26. BLACK	WATER	ICE	VELVET	DOWN	FALL
27. BUT	SO	TAR	LID	ICE	NATION
28. DOOR	SEE	NOT	LAMB	WAY	LAMP
29. ON	CELL	SEED	SIZE	LING	OUT
30. LIE	HAND	EAR	MAN	WIG	HAT

Write in the brackets a word that rhymes with the second word and has a similar meaning to the first word.

Look at this example.   SICK MILL (____ILL____)

31. PIECE   IT   (_____)

32. TUG   SCHOOL   (_____)

33. WORK   SOIL   (_____)

In the sentences below five words are missing. Choose the most appropriate words from the lists below. One word from list A fills the space at A, one word from list B fills the space at B and so on.

Underline the word you choose.

The school children played happily in the (A) as the teacher sat at his desk. It was the last day of (B) and today the children would be breaking up for their Christmas Holidays. The (C) of Christmas made all the children very (D). They hoped that soon Santa would come and deliver all his (E).

34. A	35. B	36. C	37. D	38. E
CORRIDOR	DECEMBER	FEAR	LONELY	REINDEER
DOORWAY	WEEK	THOUGHT	GOOD	GIFT
CLASSROOM	ALL	PAIN	TIRED	SNOW
GARAGE	HOLIDAYS	NOISE	EXCITED	DWARFS
HALL	TERM	SADNESS	ANXIOUS	CAKE

Two words inside the brackets have similar meanings to the words outside the brackets. Underline the TWO words each time.

Look at this example: horse, pig, cat   (falcon, <u>mouse</u>, snake, trout, <u>badger</u>)

39. walk   step   march   (parade fall paddle stride fly)

40. reservoir   cistern   panel   (tank sump water collect rain)

41. cod   mackeral   haddock   (shark pike herring whiting whale)

42. oak   chestnut   sycamore   (pine elm beech larch fir)

In the diagrams below each of the small rectangles are the same size.
What fraction of each diagram is shaded?

(_____)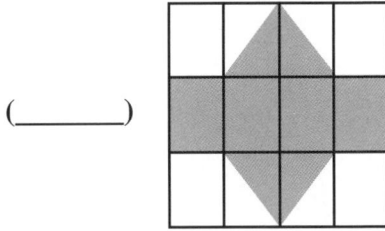

44. (_____)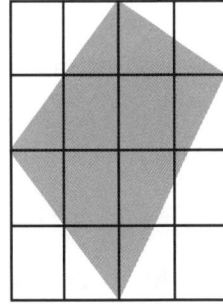

45. (_____)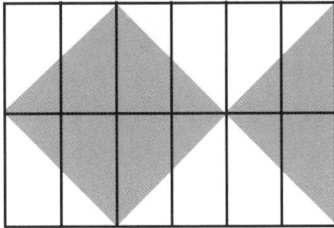

In a certain code some words are written as follows. (The alphabet is printed to help you.)

A B C D E F G H I J K L M N O P Q R S T U V W X Y Z

SMILED	is written as	WQMPIH
TOWEL	is written as	XSAIP
CHAIR	is written as	GLEMV

Write the following words in code.

46. BOOKLET   (_____) 47. MONOLITH (_____)

48. PANIC   (_____)

What are these coded words in English?

49. FEOIVC   (_____) 50. QEGLMRI (_____)

51. STIVIXXE   (_____)

A television programme began at 16.55 and lasted for 55 minutes. Sam missed the first 15 minutes but saw the rest of the programme.

52. At what time did Sam begin to watch?   (_____)

53. At what time did the programme end?   (_____)

54. How long did Sam watch for?   (_____)

In questions 55 - 60 the three words A, B and C are in alphabetical order. The word at B is missing and you are given a dictionary definition instead. Write the correct word in the space.

Look at this Example: A)   **FLAP**

B)   **(_ FLARE__) Distress signal from a boat.**

C)   **FLASH**

A)   PHOTO

55. B)   (_ _ _ _ _ _)   A group of words.

C)   PHRENOLOGY

A)   URAL

56. B)   (_ _ _ _ _)   Belonging to a city.

C)   URCHIN

A)   TIGHT

57. B)   (_ _ _ _)   Slab of baked clay for covering roofs.

C)   TILL

A)   PORPOISE

58. B)   (_ _ _ _ _ _ _ _)   Breakfast food, oatmeal boiled in water.

C)   PORT

A)   THAN

59. B)   (_ _ _ _ _)   To express gratitude.

C)   THAT

A)   OUT

60. B)   (_ _ _ _)   Egg shaped.

C)   OVEN

Six towns A, B, C, D, E and F are at the points numbered 1-6 but not in that order. The arrow points to the North.

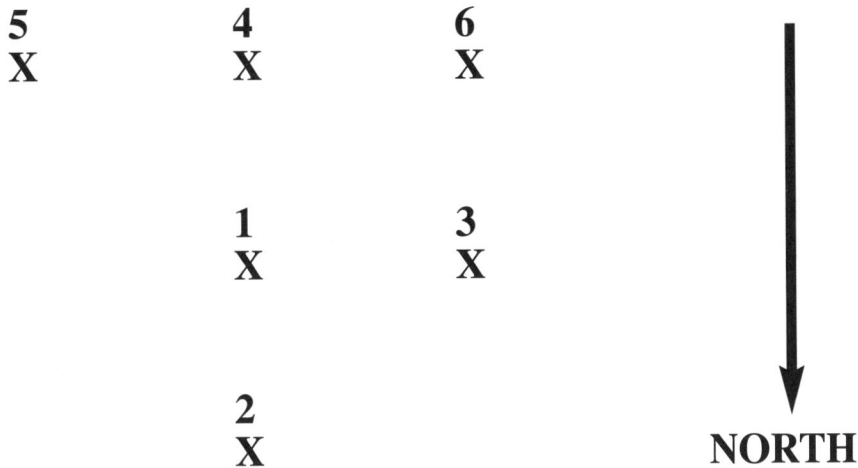

```
  5        4        6
  X        X        X           │
                                │
           1        3           │
           X        X           │
                                │
                                │
           2                    ▼
           X                 NORTH
```

Only one town is further North than towns A and C and this is not town D. Town B is due East of town F and due South of another town, which is not town C.

61. Which town is at point number 1?   (_____)

62. Which town is at point number 2?   (_____)

63. Which town is at point number 3?   (_____)

64. Which town is at point number 4?   (_____)

65. Which town is at point number 5?   (_____)

66. Which town is at point number 6?   (_____)

The words below and those in the lists are alike in some way. Write the letter of the list that each word belongs to in the brackets. Each letter may be used only once.

A	B	C	D	E
CASHEW	PLUTO	SPHERE	RICE	ALASKA
ALMOND	MINNIE	ORB	WHEAT	NEBRASKA
BRAZIL	MICKEY	BALL	BARLEY	HAWAII

67. GLOBE   (_____)

68. MILLET   (_____)

69. UTAH   (_____)

70. PEANUT   (_____)

71. DUMBO   (_____)

In each question 72 - 75 the numbers in the second column are formed from the numbers in the first column by using a certain rule. A different rule is used in each question.
Put the correct answer opposite the arrow.

72. 9 ———→ 35   73. 2.55 ———→ 4.20

     11 ———→ 41   5.35 ———→ 7.00

     7 ———→ 29   4.80 ———→ 6.45

     4 ———→ (_____)   1.35 ———→ (_____)

74. 3 ———→ 18   75. 3.50 ———→ 1.45

     5 ———→ 34   4.10 ———→ 2.05

     7 ———→ 58   6.15 ———→ 4.10

     9 ———→ (_____)   5.60 ———→ (_____)

Using the numbers 2, 7, 5 and 6 once only in each question fill in the spaces in any way which makes the statements correct.

76. (_____ + _____ − _____) X _____ = 24

77. (_____ + _____) − (_____ + _____) = 4

78. (_____ + _____ + _____) ÷ _____ = 3

79. (_____ X _____) + (_____ X _____) = 47

80. (_____ X _____) + (_____ + _____) = 39

Complete these sequences, the alphabet is printed to help you.

A B C D E F G H I J K L M N O P Q R S T U V W X Y Z

81. C,   F,   H,   K,   M   (_____)

82. BZV   FXU,   JVT,   NTS,   (_____)

83. S,   T,   R,   U,   Q,   V   (_____)

84. T,   R,   N,   H,   (_____)

85. M,   O,   K,   Q,   I,   S   (_____)

TEST 14

SCORE _____

1. Which letter appears the same number of times in the words DECISION and KESTREL?　　　　　　　　　　　　　　(_____)

2. Which letter occurs twice as often in NARCISSISM as it does in STOCKIST?　　(_____)

3. Which letter occurs less often in COMMISSION than in CLASSICAL?　　(_____)

4. In a garden there are three types of flowers. One third of them are roses. A quarter of the rest are carnations. There are 30 asters in the garden. How many carnations are there?　　　　　　　　(_____)

5. Tom has 45p. If John had 12p more he would have the same as Peter. If Tom spent one third of his money he would also have the same as Peter. How much does John have?　　　　　　　　(_____)

In the questions below TWO words must change places so that the sentences make sense. Underline the TWO words that must change places.

Look at this example:　　　The <u>wood</u> was made of <u>table</u>.

6. The girl pavement a cat on the drew.

7. A pound pond fell into a coin.

8. Minor fog caused many dense accidents.

9. Without failed the radio batteries to work.

10. The clock was slow six minutes nearly this morning.

11. I help already done it without any have.

The table below gives some information about the addition of numbers in the left hand column to numbers in the top row.

Complete the table.

	+	7.6		5.8
12				
13. 14. 15.			9.7	
16. 17.	3.4		11.2	

In each question write in the brackets one letter which will complete both the word in front of the brackets and the word after the brackets.

Look at this example.   ROA (D) OOR.

18. ACOR   (   )   ASTY   19. EMI   (   )   URF

20. SING   (   )   ACH   21. PATI   (   )   ATH

22. SPIR   (   )   QUAL   23. VER   (   )   ULB

In each line below a word from the left-hand group joins one from the right-hand group to make a new word. The left-hand word comes first.
Underline the chosen words.

Look at this example: CORN <u>FARM</u> TIME   OVER   FIELD   <u>YARD</u>

24.	GET	REST	OFF	FULL	LESS	HER
25.	OR	TRY	SIN	FARE	RING	DEAL
26.	FUR	MET	MORE	HOD	ALL	LEG
27.	CAB	SIT	TRIP	PET	LET	ILL
28.	MIST	OR	CAN	BUT	ERR	RUST
29.	ART	LET	SEA	PING	SON	HER

In the following questions a letter can be taken from the first word and put into the second word to form TWO new words. Write both NEW words.

Look at this Example: THEN TANK (TEN) (THANK)

The H moves from THEN to TANK and makes the new words TEN and THANK.

30.	PAINT	NOSE	(_____)	(_____)
31.	MORE	PAPER	(_____)	(_____)
32.	TAINT	NET	(_____)	(_____)
33.	FACTORY	FLING	(_____)	(_____)
34.	TABLE	GARAGE	(_____)	(_____)
35.	DINNER	DOOR	(_____)	(_____)

Five patients, a man, woman, boy, girl and baby are waiting to see a doctor. The girl is behind the baby but before the boy. The man is before the woman and she is one before the last. The girl is behind the man but he is not first.

36. First. (_____)

37. Second. (_____)

38. Third. (_____)

39. Fourth. (_____)

40. Fifth. (_____)

In the sentences below there are 6 words missing. From the lists A to F choose the MOST SUITABLE words to complete the sentences. Choose a word from list A to fill space A, a word from list B to fill space B and so on. Underline the chosen word in each group.

The unicorn is an (A) animal that never lived. It was (B) to have the body of a horse with a single horn (C) the middle of its forehead. It was said that a unicorn could be (D) if someone stood in front of a tree and (E) aside as it charged. The horn would then become (F) in the tree.

41. A	42. B	43. C	44. D	45. E	46. F
FOOLISH	MEANT	AT	FOUND	WENT	SCRAPED
EXTINCT	ONLY	BESIDE	FRIGHTENED	WALKED	STUCK
IMAGINARY	INTENDED	OVER	CAUGHT	JUMPED	BENT
FUNNY	ALWAYS	IN	DISCOVERED	HOPPED	SHARPENED
SAVAGE	SUPPOSED	BEHIND	ANGERED	STOOD	SCORED

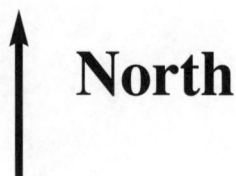

North

*47

*48   *49

*50   *51

*52

The positions of 6 towns are shown.
The towns are A, B, C, D, E and F.

Town F is further to the north than town E but is not the most northerly town.

B is directly south of one town and directly west of another.

Town A is south-east of C which is south-west of another town.

In the brackets enter the letter for each town.

47. (_____)   48.   (_____)   49.   (_____)

50. (_____)   51.   (_____)   52.   (_____)

WAIT	HAM	LACK	VIEW	OFF	TRAY	BEE
MOAN	LIAR	MIGHT	TONGUE	ONE		

From the list above choose a word which rhymes with each of the following.
Write the rhyming words in the brackets.

53. WHACK   (_____)   54.   CHOIR   (_____)

55. FREIGHT (_____)   56.   COUGH   (_____)

57. PSALM   (_____)   58.   QUEUE   (_____)

59. BONE   (_____)   60.   QUAY   (_____)

Complete the following sequences. The alphabet is printed to help you.

A B C D E F G H I J K L M N O P Q R S T U V W X Y Z

61. B   D   G   K   P   (_____)

62. A   D   F   I   K   (_____)

63. CZE   DYF   EXG   FWH   (_____)

64. EXF   HUI   KRL   NOO   (_____)

65. DWL   MEX   YNF   GZO   (_____)

66. ZA   CU   QF   JN   (_____)

67. AB   IJ   OP   ST   (_____)

In a code 2 3 4 6 1 and 1 2 3 4 5 represent two of the words

ROPES   PORTS   SPORT   POSER   SPORE.

Write each word in code.

68. ROPES   (_____)

69. PORTS   (_____)

70. SPORT   (_____)

71. POSER   (_____)

72. SPORE   (_____)

Decode the followiing.

73. 2 4 3 6 5 1 6   (_____)

74. 4 5 1 3 4 6   (_____)

75. 2 3 1 6 5 4 1   (_____)

The diagram below is made up of two triangles, a rhombus, a square, a rectangle and a parallelogram. By joining the points F I J, one of the triangles is made.

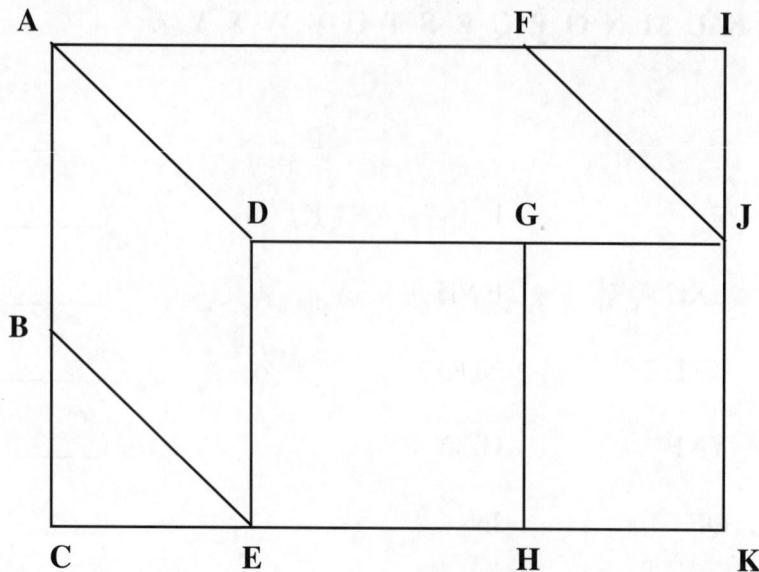

76. Which points join together to make up the other triangle?   (_____)

77. Which points join together to make up the square?   (_____)

78. Which points join together to make up the rhombus?   (_____)

79. Which points join together to make up the rectangle?   (_____)

80. Which points join together to make up the parallelogram?   (_____)

Using the numbers 3, 4, 5 and 6 ONCE ONLY in each question, fill in the spaces in any way that will make the statements correct.

Look at this example:

$$3 + 4 + 5 + 6 = 18.$$

81. (_____ + _____) − (_____ − _____)   =   6

82. (_____ + _____ + _____) X _____   =   45.

83. (_____ + _____) X (_____ − _____)   =   11.

84. (_____ X _____) − (_____ − _____)   =   11.

85. (_____ − _____) + (_____ X _____)   =   31.

TEST 15

1. Which letter occurs three times in ENCHANTING and twice in NATIONALITY? (_____)

2. Which letter appears twice in CONCENTRATES but not at all in RECESSION? (_____)

3. Which letter occurs as many times in UNYIELDING as it does in PRACTICE? (_____)

4. When three is subtracted from seven times a number the answer is 53. What is the number? (_____)

5. Twice 18 is the same as four times a number. What is the number? (_____)

A comic and two packets of crisps costs £2.95. A comic and one packet of crisps costs £2.10.

6. How much is a comic? (_____)

7. How much is a packet of crisps? (_____)

In the questions below TWO words must change places so that the sentences make sense. Underline the TWO words that must change places.

Look at this example: **The <u>wood</u> was made of <u>table</u>.**

8. There for no key was the back door.

9. Have you spend money left to any?

10. Under the strain great cord broke.

11. Running not the corridor is in allowed.

12. Was supermarket checkout every very busy.

13. Under lay scattered books the table.

The table below gives some information about the subtraction of numbers in the left-hand column from numbers in the top row.

Complete the table

	–	9.96		
14. 15.				
16. 17.	2.73		4.12	
18. 19.		5.14		3.15

In each question write in the brackets one letter which will complete both the word in front of the brackets and the word after the brackets.

Look at this example: ROA   (D)   OOR

20. MAL   ( )   ORN   21. CAS   ( )   USH

22. TAME   ( )   ORE   23. LEA   ( )   LOD

24. SOL   ( )   IGHT   25. SOD   ( )   GAIN

In each line below a word from the left-hand group joins one from the right-hand group to make a new word. The left-hand word comes first. Underline the chosen words.

Look at this example: CORN   <u>FARM</u>   TIME   OVER   FIELD   <u>YARD</u>

26. JUST	SAT	TAKE	TAN	ICE	OR
27. PAST	COMB	TOLD	AT	YOUR	MINE
28. UP	OVER	DOWN	PAIR	SIT	HOLD
29. SAD	CAT	AM	ILL	BUSH	ALE
30. BUT	WAG	TO	ON	ERR	WERE
31. USE	SAT	ACT	FULL	TING	OR

In the following questions a letter can be taken from the first word and put into the second word to form TWO new words. Write both NEW words.

Look at this example: THEN   TANK   (TEN)   (THANK)

The H moves from THEN to TANK and makes the new words TEN and THANK.

32. CANOE   SHUT   (_____)   (_____)

33. FLAKE   HALO   (_____)   (_____)

34. LEAD   SIZE   (_____)   (_____)

35. THREAT   SOW   (_____)   (_____)

36. CADGE   LAY   (_____)   (_____)

37. BALD   DARING   (_____)   (_____)

Max is 6 years older than Harry who is 3 years younger than Jacob.
Jacob is 2 years older than Thomas who is 4 years older than Theo.
Thomas is 11 and Tyler is 14.
List the boys in order from the youngest.

38. Youngest   (_____)

39.   (_____)

40.   (_____)

41.   (_____)

42.   (_____)

43. Oldest   (_____)

Groups of words are printed below. Each group is made up of words which are similar in some way.

A	B	C	D	E	F
daffodil	leopard	tango	penny farthing	kestrel	madam
daisy	puma	waltz	unicycle	hawk	tot
tulip	tiger	jive	bicycle	falcon	deed

Decide into which of the above groups the following words would fit.
Write the group letter in the brackets.
Use each letter once.

44. tandem (_____)   45. orchid (_____)

46. ewe (_____)   47. merlin (_____)

48. ballet (_____)   49. panther(_____)

In a code, words are written as shown below.

APPLE becomes **DSSOH**   **WEATHER** becomes **ZHDWKHU**

Write the following words in code. The alphabet is printed to help you.

A B C D E F G H I J K L M N O P Q R S T U V W X Y Z

50. PORCUPINE (_____)   51. WISDOM (_____)

52. EXCEPT (_____)

Decode the following words.

53. KBSKHQ (_____)   54. FRQIOLFW (_____)

55. RUJDQLF (_____)   56. UDGLVK (_____)

V, W, X, Y and Z are five books.
V and X are story books and the others are non-fiction.
X and Y are not for children but the others are.
W and Y are not paperbacks but the rest are.

57. Which hardbacked book is a non-fiction adult book?   (_____)

58. Which paperback book is a children's story book?   (_____)

59. Which adult paperback is a story book?   (_____)

60. Is there a children's paperbacked non-fiction book?   (_____)

61. Is there an adult's hardbacked story book?   (_____)

In the following questions the numbers in the second column are formed from the numbers in the first column by using the same rule. Put the correct answer in the brackets for each question.

62.
1 $\longrightarrow$ 6
3 $\longrightarrow$ 12
6 $\longrightarrow$ 21
9 $\longrightarrow$ (____)

63.
11 $\longrightarrow$ 25
8 $\longrightarrow$ 19
5 $\longrightarrow$ 13
0 $\longrightarrow$ (____)

64.
2 $\longrightarrow$ 5
6 $\longrightarrow$ 15
8 $\longrightarrow$ 20
11 $\longrightarrow$ (____)

65.
1 $\longrightarrow$ 5
4 $\longrightarrow$ 20
6 $\longrightarrow$ 40
7 $\longrightarrow$ (____)

66.
4 $\longrightarrow$ 1
10 $\longrightarrow$ 4
16 $\longrightarrow$ 7
12 $\longrightarrow$ (____)

67.
2 $\longrightarrow$ 3
6 $\longrightarrow$ 9
10 $\longrightarrow$ 15
14 $\longrightarrow$ (____)

**In each of the following questions 3 words are in alphabetical order.
The second word has not been written but its meaning is given.
Decide what the second word should be each time and write it in the
brackets. Each dash in the brackets represents a letter.**

Look at this example:

**CROSS
(CROWD)   a large group of people.
CRUEL**

NEWT
68. (_ _ _ _ _ _)   to take small bites.
NICKNAME

TEXTILE
69. (_ _ _ _ _)   upper part of leg.
TIDAL

FOAM
70. (_ _ _ _ _)   adjust to get a clear image.
FOUNDATION

SCREEN
71. (_ _ _ _ _ _ _ _)   write in a careless way.
SCRUB

MAMMAL
72. (_ _ _ _ _ _ _)   large dwelling house.
MARCH

WEASEL
73. (_ _ _ _ _)   mammal which lives in the sea.
WHEEL

3

12

5

11   6   2
              8   9   1

10   4   13

7

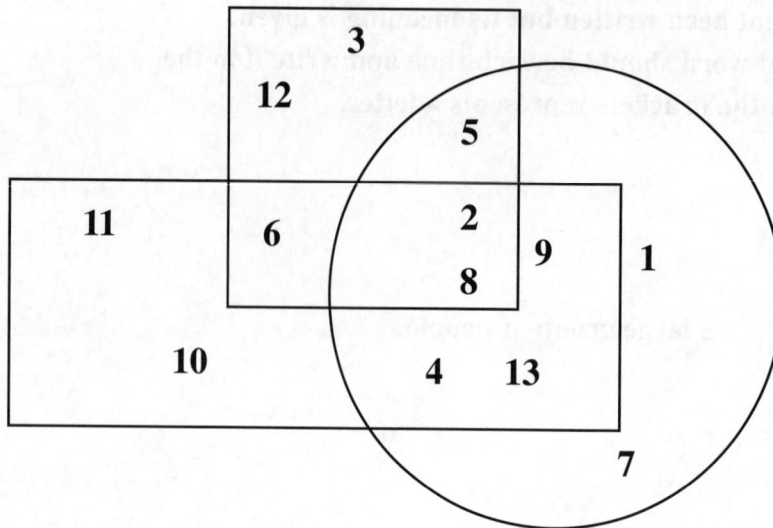

The following questions are about the numbers in the diagram above.

74. Which numbers appear in all three figures?   (_____)

75. Which number is in both the circle and square but not in the rectangle?   (_____)

76. Which numbers are in both the circle and rectangle but not in the square?   (_____)

77. Find the sum of all the numbers which appear in one figure only.   (_____)

78. Take the sum of the numbers that are in the square, but not the rectangle,
    from the sum of the numbers that are in the circle but not the square.   (_____)

79. Take the sum of the numbers that are in the circle, but not the rectangle or
    square, from the sum of the numbers that are in the rectangle, but not the
    circle or square.   (_____)

In the questions below give the next number in each series.

80.	37	21	13	9	7	(_____)
81.	1.9	3.7	5.5	7.3	9.1	(_____)
82.	1	8	27	64	125	(_____)
83.	3	8	18	38	78	(_____)
84.	2.75	4	5.25	6.5	7.75	(_____)
85.	(2,6)	(5,10)	(8,14)	(11,18)		(_____ , _____)

TEST 16

1. Which letter occurs twice in CRENELLATED but once in CREDENTIALS?   (_____)

2. Which letter occurs once in HARMONIOUS, once in LIBERATE but not at all in MELANCHOLY or in LIKE?   (_____)

3. Which letter, which occurs more than once, occurs as often in PRIVILEGED as it does in PROCEDURE?   (_____)

4. Half of a number is three quarters of 12. What is twice that number?   (_____)

5. Share 36 apples among Dylan, Toby and Noah in such a way that for every 3 apples Dylan gets, Noah gets 2, and Toby gets 4. How many apples does Toby get?   (_____)

In the questions below TWO words must change places so that the sentence makes sense. Underline the TWO words that must change places.

Look at this example: The <u>wood</u> was made of <u>table</u>.

6. Their pupils sat quietly at the desks.

7. In sails fluttered gently the the breeze.

8. Some fins have spiky fish on their backs.

9. David was unable and sick to attend school.

10. Tropical cattle are being cleared to raise forests on the land.

The table below gives some information about the subtraction of numbers in the left-hand column from those in the top row.

Complete the table correctly using only the numbers given.

5.7,   4.9,   7.3,   7.1,   1.6

	5.7	4.9	7.3	7.1	1.6
11.	-	7.8		12.0	
12, 13.		2.9	2.4		
14, 15.		6.2		10.4	

In each question below one letter can be removed from the word in the first column and put into the word in the second column to give two new words. The order of the letters is not changed.
Look at this example:

THINS   TOUT   (THIN)   (STOUT)

16. SHOUT   STOP   (_____) (_____)

17. THREAD   SOP   (_____) (_____)

18. HEARD   SET   (_____) (_____)

19. BEAR   OUGHT   (_____) (_____)

20. SPORT   ANTS   (_____) (_____)

In each line below write in the brackets one letter which completes the word in front of and the word after the brackets.

Look at this example: ROA (D) OOR

Here D completes ROAD and begins DOOR.

21. MOS   (____)   IREN

22. NEX   (____)   APER

23. PYLO   (____)   AIL

24. DEPRIV   (____)   URASIA

25. INSER   (____)   AN

In each line below underline TWO words, ONE from each side, which together make ONE correctly spelt word. The word on the left always comes first. Look at this example:

BLACK	ALL	TOP		AND	**BIRD**	BOY
26. ALL	IN	BY		SCORE	SCRIBE	PORT
27. NO	IF	NOW		YES	ON	SO
28. BY	AT	BUTTER		CYCLE	LOST	CUP
29. SAT	UP	SO		BY	URN	GASP
30. PATH	PASS	PART		OLD	PAT	AGE

Write in the brackets a word that rhymes with the second word and has a similar meaning to the first word.

Look at this example: SICK   MILL   (__ILL__)

31. AEROPLANE   MET   (_____)

32. DOG   SOUND   (_____)

33. DISCOVER   LINED   (_____)

In a certain code CHRISTMAS is written as AFPGQRKYQ.
Write the following words in code. The alphabet is printed to help you.

A B C D E F G H I J K L M N O P Q R S T U V W X Y Z   Code

34. BEFORE   (_____)

35. DANGER   (_____)

36. NAPKIN   (_____)

What do these coded words represent?

37. EPMSN   (_____)

38. CKCPEC   (_____)

39. AYJASJYRC   (_____)

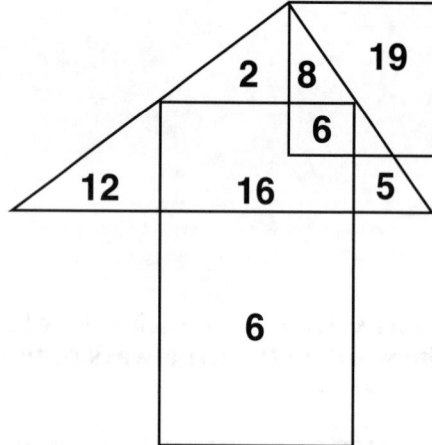

Questions 40-44 are about the above diagram which is made from a square, a rectangle and a triangle.

40. Which number is in all three shapes?   (_____)

41. From the sum of the numbers appearing only in the square, subtract the sum of the numbers appearing only in the triangle.   (_____)

42. What is the sum of all the numbers which appear in more than one shape? (_____)

43. In how many shapes does the square root of 36 appear?   (_____)

44. Add the two highest even numbers and from the total subtract all the odd numbers.   (_____)

In the questions below 2 of the words in the brackets can be made from the letters of the word outside the brackets. Underline both words.

Look at this example:

CURTAIN   (<u>TRAIN</u>   CUSTARD   STAIN   <u>RAIN</u>   TRACK)

45. TEMPERATURE   (PAPER   RATE   AFTER   MATURE   MEANT)

46. BACKWARDS   (REWARD   DWARF   RACK   DRAW   SWORD)

47. LEARNING   (NEAR   BEARING   RING   REAP   PEARL)

48. YESTERDAY   (STEEP   DREAM   READ   STEER   PESTER)

49. CONSONANTS   (COUSINS   STAND   SOON   TENTS   TONS)

50. POTATOES   (STATE   PEAS   TOTAL   STOATS   GRATE)

In the questions below underline 2 words which are closest in meaning. Underline 1 word from each set of brackets.

Look at this example:

(<u>LITTLE</u>   WASP   BIN)   (INSERT   <u>SMALL</u> RUBBISH)

51. (dig   hole   spade)   (pit   garden   fork)

52. (paper   pliers   plain)   (simple   pen   hammer)

53. (prize   money   lose)   (award   envelope   take)

54. (holiday   weekend   computer)   (days   game   vacation)

55. (ice   foam   laugh)   (lavish   froth   cold)

In questions 56-61 the three words A, B and C are in alphabetical order. The word at B is missing and you are given a dictionary definition instead. Write the correct word in the space.

Look at this example:

A) Flap
B) (__FLARE__) Distress signal from a boat.
C) FLASH

(A) PREVAIL
56. (B) (_ _ _ _ _ _ _)   To stop.
(C) PREY

(A) DUST
57. (B) (_ _ _ _ _)   Of Holland.
(C) DUTY

(A) SCRAP
58. (B) (_ _ _ _ _ _ _)   Score with claws or nails.
(C) SCRAWL

(A) MANNER
59. (B) (_ _ _ _ _)   Residence of a minister.
(C) MANUAL

(A) RINSE
60. (B) (_ _ _ _)   Trouble caused by a crowd of people.
(C) RIP

(A) AKIN
61. (B) (_ _ _ _ _)   Mechanical device to alert people.
(C) ALBINO

The words below and those in the lists are alike in some way. Write the letter of the list, that each word belongs to, in the brackets. Each letter may be used only once.

62. MAJESTIC   (_____)

63. GAGGLE   (_____)

64. PYRENEES   (_____)

65. FORTH   (_____)

66. LIME   (_____)

A.	B.	C.	D.	E.
MERSEY	SHOAL	ANDES	ELEGANT	BEECH
TYNE	FLOCK	ROCKIES	STATELY	BIRCH
THAMES	LITTER	ALPS	GRACEFUL	OAK

Complete these sequences, the alphabet is printed to help you.

A B C D E F G H I J K L M N O P Q R S T U V W X Y Z

67. A, C, G, M (____U____)

68. C, Y, F, V, I (____S____)

69. ZYY, ABB, YXX, BCC, XWW (___CDD___)

70. ZY, UT, RQ, ML, JI (____ED____)

```
                1
                X

        4       3       2
        X       X       X

        5       6
        X       X
```

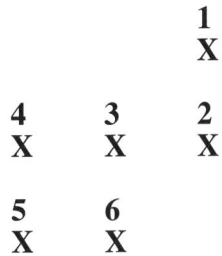

A, B, C, D, E and F are six towns at the points 1-6 but not in that order.
A is due north of C which is due east of B.
B is due south of F which is one of the two most westerly towns.
E is not furthest north.

71. Which town is at point number 1? (____D____)

72. Which town is at point number 2? (____E____)

73. Which town is at point number 3? (____A____)

74. Which town is at point number 4? (____F____)

75. Which town is at point number 5? (____B____)

76. Which town is at point number 6? (____C____)

A certain month has 5 Wednesdays and the 6th of the month is a Sunday.

77. What date is the third Thursday of the month? (____17th____)

78. How many Saturdays are there in the month? (____4____)

79. What day is the 26th of the month? (___Saturday___)

80. How many Tuesdays are there in the month? (____5____)

	Mon 5th	Tues 6th	Wed 7th	Thurs 8th	Fri 9th	Sat 10th
CUBS	57	19	76	67	73	49
BROWNIES	29	35	56	66	37	58
SCOUTS	27	26	76	47	36	114

This table shows the number of Cubs, Brownies and Scouts who went to see Peter Pan in January 2015. The dates of the days are given.

81. On which day and date were there twice as many Scouts at Peter Pan as there were Cubs on Mon 5th?   (_____)

82. On which day and date did most Brownies attend Peter Pan?   (_____)

83. On which day and date did the number of Brownies and Scouts added together equal the number of Cubs attending Peter Pan?   (_____)

84. On which day and date were there 27 less Cubs at Peter Pan than attended on Wed 7th?   (_____)

85. How many Brownies attended Peter Pan throughout the whole week?   (_____)

TEST 17

1. Which letter occurs once in MARBLE but twice in CONCRETE? (_____)

2. Which letter occurs twice in RECTANGLE but only once in TRIANGLE? (_____)

3. Which letter occurs three times in PARALLELOGRAM and three times in QUADRILATERAL? (_____)

4. Half of a number added to 8 is 7 less than 28. What is the number? (_____)

5. A pencil costs twice as much as a rubber. Two pencils and a rubber cost 50p. How much is a rubber? (_____)

In the questions below TWO words must change places so that the sentence makes sense. Underline the TWO words that must change places.

Look at this example: The <u>wood</u> was made of <u>table</u>.

6. Start at the end and finish at the beginning.

7. Learning is the key to reading.

8. Was money the locked in the drawer?

9. The racing car burst on flames into impact.

10. Only computers make mistakes, not humans.

The table below gives some information about the addition of numbers in the top row to those in the left-hand column.
Complete the table correctly using only the numbers given.

3.0,   7.6,   1.0,   11.6,   4.1

	+	7.5	5.6	
12, 13.			9.7	5.1
14, 15.	2.0	9.5		

(11. — blank column header cell in top row)

In the questions below one word can be put in front of the other
words to form four new words. Write the correct word in the brackets.
Look at this example:

FLY	**PROOF**	**WORKS**	**MAN**	**(FIRE)**
16. LOW	LONG	SIDE	HIND	(_____)
17. DOG	DOZE	FROG	FIGHT	(_____)
18. FIRE	WARDS	WASH	WATER	(_____)
19. LONG	ACHE	LIGHT	LINE	(_____)
20. WRIGHT	THING	ABLE	HOUSE	(_____)

In each question write in the brackets one letter which will complete
both the word in front of the brackets and the word after the brackets.

Look at this example: ROA (D) OOR.

21.	SHOWE	(_____)	EED
22.	HAL	(_____)	LAP
23.	PART	(_____)	ARD
24.	DUM	(_____)	ALM
25.	GAUG	(_____)	RUPT

In each line below underline TWO words, ONE from each side, which together make ONE
correctly spelt word. The word on the left always comes first.

Look at this example:

BLACK	ALL	TOP	AND	**BIRD**	BOY
26. PULL	OUT	PUT	FLAP	LET	IN
27. MAN	LAST	NOW	AND	HELP	AGE
28. CAN	CAT	CAR	HIS	CASE	HIM
29. OUT	COT	SHE	TON	RED	IN
30. AT	ON	AS	VEST	TONE	TACK

In each question below one letter can be removed from the word in the first column and put into the word in the second column to give two new words. The order of the letters is not changed.

Look at this example:

| THINS | TOUT | (THIN) | (STOUT) |

31. LATHER   ATE   (_____)   (_____)

32. HARPY   EAST   (_____)   (_____)

33. MINCE   KIT   (_____)   (_____)

34. FRILL   CHAT   (_____)   (_____)

35. POINT   HARD   (_____)   (_____)

Underline 2 words, one from each set of brackets, that have the same connection and will complete the sentence.

Look at this example:

UP is to (<u>DOWN</u> OVER LEFT)   as COME is to (START <u>GO</u> AFTER)

36. CLEAN is to (WASH SOAP DIRTY)   as HEAVY is to (LIGHT COAL LIFT)

37. FAST is to (WIN SLOW RUN)   as FACT is to (BOOK SENTENCE FICTION)

38. WHALE is to (FISH TROUT MAMMAL)   as TOAD is to (FROG RIVER AMPHIBIAN)

39. AEROPLANE is to (AIRPORT LAND ARRIVE)   as BOAT is to (WATER DOCK ANCHOR)

40. COW is to (CALF GRASS BULL)   as SOW is to (BOAR PORK GRUNT)

In the questions below one word, in bold print, has had three letters removed. These letters make a word. Write the words in the brackets.

Look at this example: We had tea in the **TING** Room   (SIT) The word is SITTING.

41. The race is **STING** at 1.00 o'clock.   (_____)

42. A wooden cross **MED** the grave.   (_____)

43. We were told to **INM** the police of any activity.   (_____)

44. In mathematics there are many 2 dimensional **SHS**.   (_____)

45. A **SE** is a useful garden tool for turning over soil.   (_____)

In the paragraph below five words are missing. Choose the most appropriate words from the lists below. One word from list A fills the space at A, one word from list B fills the space at B and so on.

Underline the word you choose.

The (**A**) entered his warm (**B**) where he has been carefully tending his young flowers. He was (**C**) to find that his assistant had failed to give the flowers (**D**) and that the loose soil was very (**E**).

46. A	47. B.	48. C.	49. D.	50. E.
PLUMBER	HALL	HAPPY	WATER	WET
FARMER	SITTING ROOM	ANNOYED	FOOD	HARD
FLORIST	HUT	LAUGHING	GRASS	COLD
DOCTOR	GREEN HOUSE	SMILING	SOIL	DAMP
JOINER	CAR	CHEERFUL	SNOW	DRY

In each question 51-56 the numbers in the second column are formed from the numbers in the first column by using a certain rule. Put the correct answer opposite the arrow. A different rule is used in each question.

51. 3.5 ⟶ 6
     6.5 ⟶ 12
     7.0 ⟶ 13
     9.5 ⟶

52. 36 ⟶ 11
     100 ⟶ 15
     144 ⟶ 17
     9 ⟶

53. 3 ⟶ 4.5
     6 ⟶ 9.0
     9 ⟶ 13.5
     15 ⟶

54. 5 ⟶ 20
     7 ⟶ 24
     8 ⟶ 26
     9 ⟶

55. 3 ⟶ 3.5
     4 ⟶ 4.0
     5 ⟶ 4.5
     10 ⟶

56. 15 ⟶ 1
     21 ⟶ 3
     12 ⟶ 0
     27 ⟶

Write in the brackets a word that rhymes with the second word and has a similar meaning to the first word.

Look at this example: SICK   MILL   (_ILL_)

57. INTERVAL   HULL   (_____)

58. UNIT   BUN   (_____)

59. STOP   FAULT   (_____)

60. BLAME   FUSE   (_____)

61. CARTON   FOX   (_____)

62. RUBBISH   TASTE   (_____)

Complete the sequences by inserting the correct numbers in the brackets.

63. 16, 24, 20, 28, 24   (_____)

64. 4.9, 6.1, 7.5, 9.1   (_____)

65. 80, 85, 95, 110, 130   (_____)

66. 625, 636, 647, 658   (_____)

67. 740, 739, 735, 726   (_____)

68. 39, 39, 34, 43, 29, 47 (_____)

69. A right-angled triangle has sides of 4cm and 8cms which touch to form a right-angle. What is half of its area?   (_____)

70. A circle can be drawn inside a square so that the circle just touches all four sides of the square. If the square has an area of 25 sq. cms. what is the radius of the circle?   (_____)

These questions are about the following shapes.

REGULAR PENTAGON,   SQUARE,
RIGHT-ANGLED TRIANGLE,   RECTANGLE.

Use this information only and answer these questions

71. Which shape or shapes do not have all internal angles the same?   (_____)

72. Which shape has most sides?   (_____)

73. Which shape or shapes could not be cut into 2 right-angled triangles using only one cut?   (_____)

74. Which shape or shapes could you not be sure would have at least one line of symmetry?   (_____)

TEST 17 PAGE 5

Questions 75 - 78 are about the lines drawn inside the squares.

A	**B**	**C**	**D**	**E**
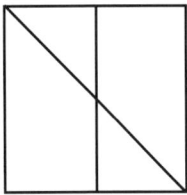	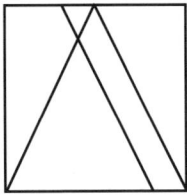	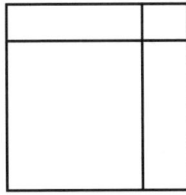	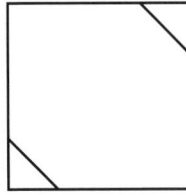	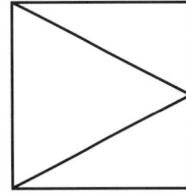

75. Name one square which has lines crossing at 45 degrees. (_____)

76,77. Name two squares with parallel lines. (_____) & (_____)

78. Name the square in which lines cross at right-angles. (_____)

**In the questions that follow letters replace numbers.
Calculate the sums and put the correct letters in the brackets.**

Look at this example:

A = 2   B = 3   C = 4   D = 8   E = 12   D x A - C   =   Letter __E__

79. A = 6   B = 3   C = 4   D = 1   E = 2   (C x D) – (C – B) = Letter ____

80. A = 6   B = 2   C = 12   D = 10   E = 5   (D – E) x (C - D) = Letter ____

81. A = 6   B = 4   C = 8   D = 7   E = 5   (C ÷ B) + (D – E) = Letter ____

82. A = 59   B = 3   C = 6   D = 2   E = 42   D x (C - B) =   Letter ____

In the questions below the words in brackets are formed from the 2 words outside the brackets.

Write the missing word in the brackets.

Look at this example:

	CAT	(TO)	OUR	RING	(GO)		OVER
83.	LIMP	(LINK)	SINK	BOWL	(	)	SEAT
84.	SNAKE	(MAKE)	SMALL	HATS	(	)	SEAL
85.	WHALE	(ABLE)	BARE	CHILDREN	(	)	MORE

TEST 18

SCORE _____

1. Which letter occurs as often in BEGINNING as it does in GRABBING? (_____)

2. Which letter appears once in UNDERSTANDING, twice in PERMISSION but not all in THOUSANDS? (_____)

3. Which letter occurs half as many times in REASONED as it does in GOVERNMENT? (_____)

4. One third of a certain number is the same as one quarter of 60. What is the number? (_____)

If Angel had 6p more he would have half as much as Alice.
Alice has 3 times as much as Freddie who is 12p short of 30p.
How much does each one have?

5. Angel. (_____)

6. Alice. (_____)

7. Freddie. (_____)

In the sentences below 2 words must change places to make the sentences sensible. Underline the TWO words. An example is shown.

The <u>wood</u> is made of <u>table</u>.

8. This time Elizabeth week next will be twelve.

9. The smoking of was in need chimney cleaning.

10. Broke the storm the clouds after up.

11. Cars park unable to were in the busy street.

12. Two boys number their coats on peg hung ten.

13. Slowly sailed ship the silently into port.

The table below gives some information about the addition of numbers in the left-hand column to numbers in the top row. Complete the table.

	+		5.5	7.6
15,16,17.	11.9			
18, 19.	8.7	17.4		

14. (row)

In each question write in the brackets one letter which will complete both the word in front of the brackets and the word after the brackets.

Here is an example: ROA (D) OOR

20. HUL (___) ERB   21. DIA (___) OAN

22. FAD (___) STATE   23. LAS (___) OME

24. TO (___) RACE   25. WAR (___) USK

In each line below a word from the left-hand group joins one from the right-hand group to make a new word. The left-hand word comes first. Underline the chosen words. An example has been done to help you.

CORN   FARM   TIME   OVER   FIELD   YARD

26. PANE   SNAP   SET   LAST   MAD   PING

27. BAR   ON   FARE   SON   GAIN   WORD

28. HEAD   OVER   FOR   TURN   ROW   DRAWER

29. PALM   FOE   OUT   THUS   LET   TIN

30. MAIN   FALL   HAS   BODY   IT   LAND

31. EVER   INN   LET   SIDE   TING   YEAR

In the following questions a letter can be taken from the first word and put into the second word to form TWO new words. Write both NEW words.

Look at this example: THEN   TANK   (TEN)   (THANK)

The H moves from THEN to TANK and makes the new words TEN and THANK.

32. DICE   PATH   (_____) (_____)

33. STREAM   CAT   (_____) (_____)

34. FLAIR   HAVE   (_____) (_____)

35. PAINT   BAT   (_____) (_____)

36. GANG   LACE   (_____) (_____)

37. TAMPER   SANK   (_____) (_____)

The letters of the word in capitals have been jumbled up. Use the clue to unjumble the letters and write the correct word in the brackets.

Look at this example: KBOO - Contains stories   (BOOK)

38. ALEYLV - A river will run in this.   (_____)

39. PENEELOV - You put a letter in this for posting.   (_____)

40. CAOTTRR - You might use this on a farm.   (_____)

41. OTBETL - A container for liquid.   (_____)

Groups of words are printed below. The groups A-F are made up of words which are similar in some way.

A	B	C	D	E	F
padre	spear	hull	post	roast	rope
minister	lance	rudder	stop	boil	string
priest	javelin	bridge	tops	fry	cord

Decide into which of the above groups the following words must fit.
Write the group letter in the brackets.

42. pots   (_____)   43. twine (_____)

44. stew   (_____)   45. pastor (_____)

46. pike   (_____)   47. keel   (_____)

In a code words are written as shown below.

ORIENTAL   becomes **ABCDEFGH**   **BUGGY**   becomes   **IJKKL**

Write the following words in code.

48. IGNORANT (_____)   49. TANGERINE (_____)

Decode the following words.

50 DEGIHD   (_____)   51. KGCDFL   (_____)

52. GFFABEDL (_____)   53. HGEKJGKD (_____)

The information below is about 4 boys W, X, Y and Z and the drinks that they like.

W and X are the only two who like both milk and lemonade.
X and Z are the only two who like both lemonade and tea.
Y and W are the only two who like both fruit juice and coffee.

54. Which drink does W not like?   (_____)

55. Who likes coffee but not lemonade?   (_____)

56. Who likes lemonade, tea and milk?   (_____)

57. Who likes lemonade but not tea?   (_____)

58. Who likes coffee and fruit juice but not milk? (_____)

59. Which drink is the most popular?   (_____)

In a month there were 4 Wednesdays. The 19th of the month was a Saturday.

60. What day was the 1st of the month?   (_____)

61. What date was the third Sunday?   (_____)

62. Which month could it be? (May, February or April)   (_____)

63. What date was the last Friday of the previous month?   (_____)

64. What day was the 20th of the previous month?   (_____)

Complete the following sequences. The alphabet is printed to help you.

A B C D E F G H I J K L M N O P Q R S T U V W X Y Z

65. A   Y   B   W   C   (_____)

66. B   E   G   J   L   (_____)

67. FL   MG   HN   OI   (_____)

68. CCX   VDD   EET   RFF   (_____)

69. BDC   EGF   HJI   KML   (_____)

70. ZRC   ESY   XTG   IUW   (_____)

In each of the following questions 3 words are in alphabetical order. The second word has not been written but its meaning is given. Decide what the second word should be each time and write it in the brackets. Each dash in the brackets represents a letter. An example is shown to help you.

CROSS

(C R O W D) a large group of people.

CRUEL

MIRROR

71. (_ _ _ _ _)   person who hoards money.

MITTEN

HASTY

72. (_ _ _ _ _ _ _) short, light axe.

HAUNT

ORANGE

73. (_ _ _ _ _)   path of a planet around the sun.

OSTRICH

STRONG

74. (_ _ _ _ _ _)   artist's work-room.

STUTTER

LANTERN

75. (_ _ _ _ _ _)   storage room for food.

LATCH

COMFORT

76. (_ _ _ _ _)   humorous, funny.

CONCEAL

Together Poppy, Lucy, Millie, Oscar and Erin have £84.
Millie has £3 less than Poppy who has £5 more than Erin.
Erin has £5 less than Lucy.
Oscar has £20 which is £2 more than Poppy.

77. How much has Poppy?   (£_____)

78. How much has Lucy?   (£_____)

79. How much has Millie?   (£_____)

80. How much has Erin?   (£_____)

Using the numbers 2, 3, 4 and 6 ONCE ONLY in each question, fill in the spaces in a way that will make the statements correct. An example is shown to help you.

2 + 3 + 4 + 6 = 15.

81. (_____ + _____) ▪ (_____ ▪ _____)   =   3.

82. (_____ + _____ + _____) X _____   =   26.

83. (_____ + _____)   X   (_____ ▪ _____)   =   8.

84. (_____ X _____)   ▪   (_____ ▪ _____)   =   8.

85. (_____ ▪ _____)   +   (_____ X _____)   =   25.

TEST 19

SCORE _____

1. Which letter appears the same number of times in the words REMEMBER and ENFORCEMENT? (_____)

2. Which letter is in the word PRESIDENT but not in the word DEPRESSION? (_____)

3. Which letter occurs twice as often in PARTICULAR as it does in SECRETARY? (_____)

4. Six times a number is four more than twice 19. What is the number? (_____)

In three years Owen will be twice as old as Seth was last year. Felix, who will be 5 next year, is 2 years younger than Seth. How old is each boy?

5. Owen (_____)

6. Seth (_____)

7. Felix (_____)

In the sentences below 2 words must change places to make the sentences sensible. Underline the TWO words. An example is shown.

The <u>wood</u> is made of <u>table</u>.

8. Tom's watch and one was a half minutes fast.

9. The aeroplane flew just above an ground.

10. The bay was in rough for fishing too.

11. I to not reach could the top shelf.

12. Always before food well chew swallowing it.

13. Peter hugged long his lost brother.

The table below gives some information about the addition of numbers in the left-hand column to numbers in the top row. Complete the table.

	+	8.7		
14,15.				
16,17.	12.6		26.4	
18,19.		18.1		20

In each question write in the brackets one letter which will complete
both the word in front of the brackets and the word after the brackets.

Look at this example: ROA (D) OOR

20. CAME ( ) ENS   21. TAR ( ) ASK

22. GE   ( ) AID   23. SCA ( ) ACK

24. FAN   ( ) ABLE   25. TAL ( ) ALM

In each line below a word from the left-hand group joins one from the
right-hand group to make a new word. The left-hand word comes first.
Underline the chosen words. An example has been done to help you.

CORN	FARM	TIME	OVER	FIELD	YARD
26. AIM	OVER	OUT	RING	PUT	TEAR
27. BAND	OR	GET	IT	GILL	BUT
28. FOR	SUM	TO	WORK	LET	WING
29. OVER	DEAD	COME	SON	LOCK	LEE
30. BE	SET	RAN	LESS	PANT	SACK
31. PORT	CORD	NO	ABLE	TAIL	HEAD

In the following questions a letter can be taken from the first word and
put into the second word to form TWO new words. Write both NEW words.

Example: THEN   TANK   (TEN)   (THANK)

The H moves from THEN to TANK and makes the new words TEN andTHANK.

32. NIECE   PACE   (_____) (_____)

33. BARON   NOSE   (_____) (_____)

34. YEAR   EARL   (_____) (_____)

35. MANAGER   HAD   (_____) (_____)

36. GAUNT   BARE   (_____) (_____)

37. PART   GEM   (_____) (_____)

Two words inside the brackets have similar meanings to words outside the brackets. Underline the TWO words each time.

Look at this example:

HORSE PIG CAT   (FALCON <u>MOUSE</u> TROUT <u>BADGER</u> SNAKE)

38. DISCUS JAVELIN HURDLES   (SPORT MARATHON SPRINT RUGBY GAMES)

39. SETTEE BENCH STOOL   (CUSHION CHAIR BED THRONE CABINET)

40. RICE OATS RYE   (GROWN BARLEY FOOD SERIAL WHEAT)

41. CHEERFUL CONTENTED GLAD   (ECSTATIC GLUM HAPPY SAD FEELINGS)

42. BAFFLING COMPLICATED CONFUSING (EASY SMART PUZZLING DIFFICULT PROBLEM)

43. PRUNE CLIP TRIM   (CUT LOP GRASS HORSE GARDEN)

In the sentences below there are 6 words missing. From the lists A to F choose the MOST SUITABLE words to complete the sentences.

Choose a word from list A to fill space A, a word from list B to fill space B and so on. <u>Underline the chosen word in each group.</u>

The power went (**A**) and I was left in darkness. I felt my way to the drawer to find a (**B**). Groping in the (**C**) I struck a light and the room was filled with a (**D**) glow. Pulling back the curtain I saw the street lights were (**E**). The fault, I decided, must be in my (**F**).

44. A	45. B	46. C	47. D	48. E	49. F
out	torch	room	little	lit	room
away	match	shadows	shiny	shattered	switch
bang	bulb	dark	blinding	off	house
off	lamp	silence	faint	out	plugs
dim	fuse	hall	piercing	broken	bulbs

The table below shows the number of people in various age groups in four villages called Sulby, Picton, Marlow and Widford.

Age group A - Up to 18 years of age.
Age group B - From 19 to 60 years of age.
Age group C - Over 60 years of age.

Age Group	SULBY	PICTON	MARLOW	WIDFORD
A	550	400	120	420
B	700	530	400	530
C	270	310	320	310

50. Which age group A, B or C has the greatest number of people?   (_____)

51. Which age group A, B or C has the smallest number of people?   (_____)

52. Which village has more than half as many people in group A as in groups B and C together?   (_____)

53. Which village has one third of its population in group A?   (_____)

54. Which village has one quarter of its population in group C?   (_____)

In the questions below give the next number in each series.

55. 2   5   11   23   (_____)

56. 8.8   7.2   5.6   4   (_____)

57. 80   63   48   35   (_____)

58. (4, 9)   (11, 23)   (18, 37)   (_____,_____)

59. (27, 3)   (21, 7)   (15, 11)   (_____,_____)

The two sets of numbers in each line go together in a similar way. Write the missing number each time.

Example: (7 ⟶ 14 ⟶ 16)   (9 ⟶ 18 ⟶ <u>20</u>)

(Double number and add 2)

60. (8 ⟶ 3 ⟶ 10)   (14 ⟶ 9 ⟶ _____)

61. (7 ⟶ 21 ⟶ 24)   (10 ⟶ 30 ⟶ _____)

62. (16 ⟶ 4 ⟶ 3)   (36 ⟶ 6 ⟶ _____)

63. (2 ⟶ 8 ⟶ 13)   (4 ⟶ 64 ⟶ _____)

64. (12 ⟶ 6 ⟶ 1)   (24 ⟶ 12 ⟶ _____)

65. (27 ⟶ 3 ⟶ 14)   (64 ⟶ 4 ⟶ _____)

In each of the following questions find a word which has a similar meaning to the left-hand word and rhymes with the right-hand word.

Look at this Example: TREMBLE   RIVER   (SHIVER)

SHIVER rhymes with RIVER and means TREMBLE.

66. MAIDEN   WHIRL   (_____)

67. RATION   FAIR   (_____)

68. FAITHFUL   CLUE   (_____)

69. CABLE   TYRE   (_____)

70. SHIP   NOTE   (_____)

71. CONSTRUCT   ACHE   (_____)

In the following questions the numbers in the second column are formed from the numbers in the first column by using the same rule. Put the correct answer in the brackets for each question.

72. 3 ——→ 8
    7 ——→ 16
    10 ——→ 22

    20 ——→ (___)

73. 12 ——→ 1
    15 ——→ 2
    24 ——→ 5

    30 ——→ (___)

74. 2 ——→ 7
    3 ——→ 26
    4 ——→ 63

    5 ——→ (___)

75. 4 ——→ 6
    7 ——→ 12
    11 ——→ 20

    24 ——→ (___)

76. 4 ——→ 3
    14 ——→ 8
    20 ——→ 11

    30 ——→ (___)

77. 2 ——→ 5
    4 ——→ 17
    7 ——→ 50

    9 ——→ (___)

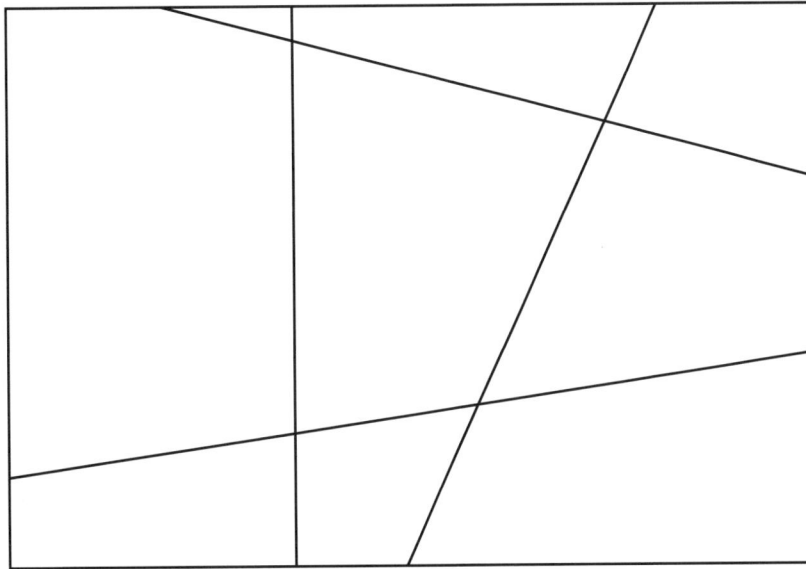

State whether the following statements about the diagram above are true or false. Write T for true or F for false in the brackets.

78. There are more than 6 right angles. (_____)

79. There are more than 6 triangles. (_____)

80. There are 3 lines parallel to one another. (_____)

81. There are 3 horizontal lines. (_____)

82. One of the lines divides the diagram into two equal pieces. (_____)

Some letters from the word in capitals have been used to make other words. Underline the TWO words that have been made each time.

Look at this example:

CONVENIENT   <u>tonic</u>   video   notion   <u>voice</u>

83. COLLABORATE: barrel   robot   elated   bear

84. DANDELION: dried   landed   panda   deal

85. MATHEMATICS: theme   tame   cheat   thermal

TEST 20

1. Which letter occurs as often in EPIDEMIC as it does in EPICURE and also occurs twice in DISCONNECT?   (_____)

2. Which letter, occurring once in GASTRONOMY, occurs twice in GASTRONOMIST and twice in GAZETTE?   (_____)

3. Which letter in GEANTICLINE occurs more than once and is closest to the end of the alphabet?   (_____)

4. When 6 is subtracted from a number it gives an answer which is 5 more than 29. What is the number?   (_____)

A cake costs 55p more than a packet of biscuits. Together they cost £3.05p.

5. How much is a cake?   (_____)

6. How much is a packet of biscuits?   (_____)

In the questions below TWO words must change places so that the sentence makes sense. Underline the TWO words that must change places.

Look at this example: The <u>wood</u> was made of <u>table</u>.

7. The neighbours that complained the music was too loud.

8. The was garage left open and unattended?

9. The sweet cake was laden with a beautiful trolley.

10. Three ambulances arrived within the minutes of the accident.

11. I could not the find word in my dictionary.

12. Air up are going fares next month.

The table below gives some information about the subtraction of numbers in the left-hand column from those in the top row. Complete the table correctly.

13. **−**		3.9
14.	4.7	2.3
15. 2.9		1.0
16,17.	2.4	

In each line below write in the brackets one letter which completes the word in front of and the word after the brackets.

Look at this example: **ROA (D) OOR**

18. RHYTH (_____) URMUR

19. SLAN (_____) HEFT

20. SHEE (_____) INTH

21. STA (_____) OLK

22. POR (_____) LOPE

23. CUR (_____) AID

TEST 20 PAGE 2

In each line below underline TWO words, ONE from each side, which together make ONE correctly spelt word. The word on the left always comes first.

Look at this example: <u>BLACK</u>   ALL   TOP   AND   <u>BIRD</u> BOY

24.	AS	AFTER	AGO	GO	TASTE	MOON
25.	SEE	SAW	SAT	TED	DING	PAY
26.	NO	SERF	OF	VICE	ALL	PUT
27.	ARE	FEAT	CUT	HIM	BIT	HER
28.	HUM	OR	RIB	BUD	AN	GAIN
29.	COT	FLAT	PORT	TEN	END	TEND

In each question below, two consecutive letters can be removed from the word in the first column and put into the word in the second column to give two new words. The order of the letters is not changed and the two consecutive letters remain together.

Look at this example: GIR<u>DLE</u>   ASH   (GIRD)   (<u>LEASH</u>)

30.	HANDLE	BED	(_____)	(_____)
31.	CARPET	HELD	(_____)	(_____)
32.	BEDROOM	IT	(_____)	(_____)
33.	PILLOW	BELL	(_____)	(_____)
34.	FLOWER	BET	(_____)	(_____)

In questions 35-40 the three words A, B and C are in alphabetical order. The word at B is missing and you are given a dictionary definition instead. Write the correct word in the space.

Look at this example:
A) FLAP
B) (FLARE) Distress signal from a boat.
C) FLASH

35. (A) NETTLE
    (B) (_ _ _ _ _ _ _) Not favouring either side.
    (C) NEVER

36. (A) BEVERAGE
    (B) (_ _ _ _ _ _) Be on one's guard.
    (C) BEWITCH

37. (A) SALAMANDER
    (B) (_ _ _ _ _ _) Fixed payment made to a person.
    (C) SALIVA

38. (A) THE
    (B) (_ _ _ _ _ _ _) A structure for showing drama.
    (C) THEIR

39. (A) PROSTRATE
    (B) (_ _ _ _ _ _ _) To guard from danger.
    (C) PROTEST

40. (A) STRIKE
    (B) (_ _ _ _ _ _) Fine cord.
    (C) STRIPE

The words below, and those in the lists, are alike in some way. Write the letter of the list that each word belongs to in the brackets. Each letter may be used only once.

A	B	C	D	E
FEZ	CROWD	QUAY	CUB	BAT
CROWN	RABBLE	DOCK	FOAL	FOX
BERET	GANG	HARBOUR	DUCKLING	HORSE

41. WHARF   (_____)

42. CYGNET   (_____)

43. TURBAN   (_____)

44. WHALE   (_____)

45. MOB   (_____)

In the following questions the letters of words have been jumbled up. A clue is given to help you each time.

Look at this example: IATSDUM **Sports ground (Stadium)**

46. ALIEMDC Examination by a doctor (_____)

47. ODELUB Twice the amount (_____)

48. RAELCST Brilliant orange-red colour (_____)

49. UKARLEWM Neither hot nor cold water (_____)

50. ENALREG High ranking army officer (_____)

51. LEPTANEH Hugh, thick skinned mammal (_____)

Using the numbers 7, 8, 5 and 4 once only in each question fill in the spaces in any way which makes the statements correct.

52. (_____ + _____ + _____) ▬ (_____) = 8

53. (_____ ▬ _____) + (_____ ▬ _____) = 6

54. _____ X (_____ + _____ + _____) = 80

55. (_____ X _____) ▬ (_____ X _____) = 3

56. (_____ ▬ _____) ▬ (_____ ▬ _____) = 0

57. (_____ + _____ ▬ _____) X _____ = 24

A, B, C and D are four shops.
Only A and D are open late in the evenings and are closed on Sundays.
Only B and C have self-service and have a sale on at present.
Only D and B are closed on Sunday and have self-service.

58. Which shop is closed on Sunday and is not self-service? (_____)

59. Which self-service shop has a sale but closes on Sunday? (_____)

60. Which shop closes early and on Sunday? (_____)

61. Which shop opens on Sunday and has a sale? (_____)

62. Could you buy something in shop D late on a Sunday? (_____)

63. Is there a self-service shop open late? (_____)

	BREAM	ROACH	PIKE
ENGLAND	65	44	132
IRELAND	127.5	32.5	40
FRANCE	70	122.6	63.75

The above table shows the weight (in kgs.) of three different types of fish caught by three fishing teams in a fishing contest.

64. Which team caught half the weight in pike as Ireland caught in bream? (_____)

65. Which team caught 3 times as much weight in pike as England caught in roach? (_____)

66. Which team caught 1/5th of its total weight of fish in pike? (_____)

67. Which team's catch of bream was twice as heavy as Ireland's catch of roach? (_____)

68. Which team caught 3/4's as much again in bream as Ireland caught in pike? (_____)

Complete these sequences by inserting the correct letter(s) or number(s) in the brackets. The alphabet is printed to help you.

A B C D E F G H I J K L M N O P Q R S T U V W X Y Z

69. 121, 81, 49, 25   (_____)

70. 104, 156, 208, 260   (_____)

71. 4.70, 7.05, 9.40, 11.75   (_____)

72. B, D, G, I   (_____)

73. DBC, GEF, JHI, MKL   (_____)

74. XBD, FCV, TDH, JER   (_____)

Two words inside the brackets have similar meanings to the words outside the brackets. Underline the TWO words each time.

Look at this example: Horse, Pig, Cat   (falcon, <u>mouse</u>, snake, trout, <u>badger</u>)

75.	Hammer	Saw	Screwdriver	(nail,	spanner,	pliers,	fork,	sharpener)
76.	Tennis	Rugby	Football	(golf	badminton	archery	swimming	netball)
77.	Kitten	Joey	Piglet	(bull	tadpole	boar	mare	calf)
78.	Groom	Ring	Service	(home	curtain	bride	bouquet	garden)
79.	Wool	Fur	Mink	(cotton	nylon	silk	leather	polyester)
80.	Stockholm	London	Washington	(Dublin	Venice	Manchester	Paris	Glasgow)

In a certain code

DISCOUNT is written as HMWGSYRX
JANUARY   is written as NERYEVC
MATCHES   is written as QEXGLIW

The alphabet is printed to help you.

A B C D E F G H I J K L M N O P Q R S T U V W X Y Z

What are these words in code?

81. POLISH   (_____)

82. SECRET   (_____)

83. TALKING   (_____)

Decode these words.

84. IRKMRI   (_____)

85. EYXLSV   (_____)

Answers to Test 11

1. N
2. A
3. E
4. 8
5. 10
6. 5
7. 5
8. FAN ... CAR
9. RAIN ... TOP
10. SAILED ... LIFTED
11. NOTE ... TORN
12. DINNER ... ARE
13. 3.8
14. 3
15. 3.4
16. 2.6
17. M
18. R
19. Y
20. P
21. G
22. D or T
23. K
24. HG
25. BCD
26. ON
27. 7.5
28. 9
29. 2
30. 14.2
31. FOR ... SAKE
32. DAM ... PEN
33. JERK ... IN
34. PASS ... ABLE
35. TAB ... LET
36. MAN ... OR
37. MISERABLE
38. HUDDLED
39. WARM
40. SEARCH
41. 4
42. 7
43. 2
44. 3
45. 1
46. 7.5 or 7 1/2
47. 7
48. -1
49. EMEND
50. EMERGE
51. EMERY
52. ENAMEL
53. ENCLOSE
54. 2.00
55. 2.05
56. 2.40
57. LATER ... THICK
58. FORD ... BAIT
59. RISE ... KNIT
60. LANE ... CHARM
61. THEM ... GALLERY
62. MAZE ... NOISE
63. FIST ... CROW
64. CAPS ... MARROW
65. SOUTH
65. SOUTH
67. NORTH
63. HEAT
69. REAL
70. ROOM
71. DOES
72. THEM
73. PEAL
74. D
75. C
76. A and E
77. 10
78. MID
79. GUN
80. DOWN
81. OVER
82. 18   2X
83. 6   Sq root X-1
84. 36   2X + 2
85. 2   Half of (X-2)

Answers to Test 12

1. N
2. R
3. W
4. 27
5. 13p
6. TELEVISION ... CHILD
7. PICTURE ... FRAMED
8. SUN ... PAINT
9. PROGRAM ... OPERATROR
10. PRESENT ... MOTHER
11. 5.1
12. 2.5
13. 22.7
14. 27.3
15. 35.95
16. 28.75
17. N
18. G
19. E
20. R
21. L
22. HALL ... HULL*
23. PINE ... PANE*
24. FACE ... LACE*
25. HERB ... HERD*
26. CHIP ... SHIP*
27. NOT ... ICE
28. BOOK ... CASE
29. PAGE ... ANT
30. STIR ... RING
31. SUIT ... OR
32. VICAR ... AGE
33. PENCILS
34. CALCULATOR
35. ISLAND
36. PADDOCK
37. WEAPON
38. REPLY
39. RAISE
40. MOB
41. EXPLODED
42. OCTOBER
43. GASPED
44. CASCADE
45. DARK
46. TEAT ... PRINT
47. FIN ... DRUM
48. VICE ... OWING
49. GASH ... LINEN
50. BACK ... RULE
51. 00.09 (24HR CLOCK)
52. 0.55 (-0.9)
53. 62,11 (+7,-8)
54. 47(+5,7,9 ETC)
55. 4 (÷by 4)
56. (8X6) - (5X4)*
57. (6+5+8) X 4*
58. (8-5)-(6-4)*
59. (8+5)X(6+4)*
60. (6X4)-(8+5)*
61. ANXIOUS
62. PLAGUE
63. FOUNTAIN
64. HIRE
65. JACKAL
66. MOUTH
67. 65 (XSQ + 1)
68. 35 (X + ½x)
69. 35 (XSQ - 1)
70. 272 (3X+2)
71. B,C,E**
72. B,C
73. D,E
74. D
75. C
76. A
77. C
78. E
79. C
80. A
81. 48 Kuna
82. 100 Kuna
33. 220 Kuna
84. £17.50
85. 164 Kuna

* There are other possibilities.
** Other combinations may
    work.

These are the answers to tests 11 - 15 of graded tests. A child who has not previously attempted questions of this type may have difficulty with the first few tests. However, research shows that a child's ability to handle and understand these questions generally increases with practice.

website: www.learningtogether.co.uk   E-mail: smcconkey@learningtogether.co.uk   Learning Together 11+ Publishers Ltd, 18 Shandon Park, Belfast BT5 6NW Phone/fax 028 90402086

Answers to Test 13

1. I
2. L
3. I
4. 19
5. 32
6. GRATE FIRE
7. PAPERS ROOMS
8. BEEN HAD
9. BY IN
10. OF A
11. 1.08
12. 11.3
13. 2.88
14. 0.08
15. 1.16
16. T
17. E
18. P
19. L
20. N
21. BAKE BRASS
22. LED MOIST
23. RANGE GRUB
24. POND HOUSING
25. CONE PANEL/PLANE
26. WATER FALL
27. CAR NATION/SO LID
28. DOOR WAY
29. SEED LING
30. EAR WIG
31. BIT
32. PULL
33. TOIL
34. CLASSROOM
35. TERM
36. THOUGHT
37. EXCITED
38. GIFTS
39. PARADE STRIDE
40. TANK SUMP
41. HERRING WHITING
42. ELM BEECH
43. 1/2
44. 1/2
45. 1/2
46. FSSOPIX
47. QSRSPMXL
48. TERMG
49. BAKERY
50. MACHINE
51. OPERETTA
52. 17.10
53. 17.50
54. 40 MINS
55. PHRASE
56. URBAN
57. TILE
58. PORRIDGE
59. THANK
60. OVAL
61. A
62. E
63. C
64. B
65. D
66. F
67. C
68. D
69. E
70. A
71. B
72. 20 (3X + 8)
73. 3.0 (+1.65)
74. 90 (XSQ. +9)
75. 3.55 (-2.05)
76. (2+7-5) X 6*
77. (7+5) - (2+6)*
78. (7+6+2) ÷ 5*
79. (7X5) + (2X6)*
80. (5X6) + (2+7)

Answers to Test 14

1. S
2. I
3. C
4. 10
5. 18
6. PAVEMENT DREW
7. POND COIN
8. MINOR DENSE
9. FAILED BATTERIES
10. SLOW NEARLY
11. HELP HAVE
12. 7.8
13. 1.9
14. 9.5
15. 7.7
16. 11.0
17. 9.2
18. N
19. T
20. E
21. O
22. E
23. B
24. REST LESS
25. OR DEAL
26. MET HOD
27. TRIP LET
28. MIST RUST
29. SEA SON
30. PANT NOISE
31. ORE PAMPER
32. TINT NEAT
33. FACTOR FLYING
34. TALE GARBAGE
35. DINER DONOR
36. BABY
37. MAN
38. GIRL
39. WOMAN
40. BOY
41. IMAGINARY
42. SUPPOSED
43. IN
44. CAUGHT
45. JUMPED
46. STUCK
47. D
48. C
49. F
50. B
51. A
52. E
53. LACK
54. LIAR
55. WAIT
56. OFF
57. HAM
58. VIEW
59. MOAN
60. BEE
61. V
62. N
63. GVI
64. QLR
65. PHA
66. LO
67. UV
68. 43251
69. 23461
70. 12346
71. 23154
72. 12345
73. PROTEST
74. RESORT
75. POSTERS
76. BCE*
77. DGHE*
78. ADEB*
79. GJKH*
80. AFJD
81. 5, 4, 6, 3**
82. 4, 5, 6, 3**
83. 6, 5, 4, 3**
84. 3, 4, 6, 5**
85. 4, 3, 6, 5**

Answers to Test 15

1. N
2. T
3. E
4. 8
5. 9
6. 85p
7. £1.25
8. FOR WAS
9. SPEND
10. THE GREAT
11. NOT IN
12. WAS EVERY
13. UNDER BOOKS
14. 6.85
15. 7.97
16. 7.23
17. 5.24
18. 4.82
19. 2.03
20. T
21. H
22. S
23. P
24. E
25. A
26. JUST ICE
27. COMB AT
28. UP HOLD
29. AM BUSH
30. WAG ON
31. ACT OR
32. CANE SHOUT
33. FAKE HALLO
34. LAD SEIZE
35. TREAT SHOW
36. CAGE LADY
37. BAD DARLING
38. THEO
39. HARRY
40. THOMAS
41. JACOB
42. TYLER
43. MAX
44. D
45. A
46. F
47. E
48. C
49. B
50. SRUFXSLQH
51. ZLVGRP
52. HAFHSW
53. HYPHEN
54. CONFLICT
55. ORGANIC
56. RADISH
57. Y
58. V
59. X
60. YES
61. NO
62. 30   3X + 3
63. 3   2X + 3
64. 27.5   ½X × 5
65. 53   XSQ + 4
66. 5   (X÷2) - 1
67. 21   1.5X
68. NIBBLE
69. THIGH
70. FOCUS
71. SCRIBBLE
72. MANSION
73. WHALE
74. 2, 8
75. 5
76. 4, 9, 13
77. 44
78. 14
79. 13
80. 6
81. 10.9
82. 216
83. 158
84. 9
85. 14, 22

*THERE ARE OTHER POSSIBILITIES   ** OTHER COMBINATIONS MAY WORK

Answers to Test 16

1. L
2. R
3. E
4. 36
5. 16
6. THEIR | THE
7. IN | THE
8. FINS | FISH
9. UNABLE | SICK
10. CATTLE | FORESTS
11. 7.3
12. 4.9
13. 7.1
14. 1.6
15. 5.7
16. SHUT | STOOP
17. TREAD | SHOP
18. HERD | SEAT
19. EAR | BOUGHT
20. SORT | PANTS
21. S
22. T
23. N
24. E
25. T
26. IN | SCRIBE
27. NO | ON
28. BUTTER | CUP
29. SAT | URN
30. PASS | AGE
31. JET
32. HOUND
33. FIND
34. ZCDMPC
35. BYLECP
36. LYNIGL
37. GROUP
38. EMERGE
39. CALCULATE
40. 6
41. 0
42. 30
43. 3
44. 4
45. RATE | MATURE
46. RACK | DRAW
47. NEAR | RING
48. READ | STEER
49. SOON | TONS
50. STATE | PEAS
51. HOLE | PIT
52. PLAIN | SIMPLE
53. PRIZE | AWARD
54. HOLIDAY | VACATION
55. FOAM | FROTH
56. PREVENT
57. DUTCH
58. SCRATCH
59. MANSE
60. RIOT
61. ALARM
62. D
63. B
64. C
65. A
66. E
67. U
68. S
69. CDD
70. ED
71. D
72. E
73. A
74. F
75. B
76. C
77. 17TH
78. 4
79. SAT
80. 5
81. SAT 10TH
82. THURS 8TH
83. FRI 9TH
84. SAT 10TH
85. 281

Answers to Test 17

1. E
2. E
3. A
4. 26
5. 10P
6. END | BEGINNING
7. LEARNING | READING
8. MONEY | THE
9. ON | INTO
10. COMPUTERS | HUMANS
11. 1.0
12. 4.1
13. 11.6
14. 7.6
15. 3.0
16. BE
17. BULL
18. BACK
19. HEAD
20. PLAY
21. R or D
22. F
23. Y
24. P or B
25. E
26. OUT | LET
27. MAN | AGE
28. CAR | CASE
29. COT | TON
30. AT | TACK
31. LATHE/LATER | RATE/HATE
32. HARP | YEAST
33. MICE | KNIT
34. FILL | CHART
35. PINT | HOARD
36. DIRTY | LIGHT
37. SLOW | FICTION
38. MAMMAL | AMPHIBIAN
39. AIRPORT | DOCK
40. BULL | BOAR
41. ART
42. ARK
43. FOR
44. APE
45. PAD
46. FLORIST
47. GREENHOUSE
48. ANNOYED
49. WATER
50. DRY
51. 18 (2 x – 1)
52. 8 (Square Root X + 5)
53. 22.5 (x + ½ x)
54. 28 (2 X + 10)
55. 7 (½ x + 2)
56. 5 (X ÷ 3) - 4
57. LULL
58. ONE
59. HALT
60. ACCUSE
61. BOX
62. WASTE
63. 32
64. 10.9
65. 155
66. 669
67. 710
68. 24
69. 8cm²
70. 2.5cm
71. RIGHT ANGLED TRIANGLE
72. REGULAR PENTAGON
73. REGULAR PENTAGON
74. RIGHT ANGLED TRIANGLE
75. A or B
76. B or D
77. B or D
78. C
79. B
80. D
81. B
82. C
83. BOAT
84. EATS
85. OMEN

* There may be other possible answers.

These are the answers to tests 15 - 20 of graded tests. A child who has not previously attempted questions of this type may have difficulty with the first few tests. However, research shows that a child's ability to handle and understand these questions generally increases with practice.

website: www.learningtogether.co.uk   E-mail: smcconkey@learningtogether.co.uk   Learning Together 11+ Publishers Ltd, 18 Shandon Park, Belfast BT5 6NW Phone/fax 028 90402086

Answers to Test 18

1. G
2. I
3. N
4. 45
5. 21P
6. 54P
7. 18P
8. ELIZABETH NEXT
9. OF CHIMNEY
10. BROKE AFTER
11. PARK WERE
12. NUMBER TEA
13. SAILED HUNG
14. 8.7 THE
15. 20.6
16. 17.4
17. 19.5
18. 14.2
19. 16.3
20. K
21. L
22. E or S
23. H or S
24. G or T
25. T or D or M
26. SNAP PING
27. BAR GAIN
28. OVER TURN
29. OUT LET
30. MAIN LAND
31. LET TING
32. DIE PATCH
33. STEAM CART
34. FAIR HALVE
35. PANT BAIT
36. GAG LANCE
37. TAMER SPANK
38. VALLEY
39. ENVELOPE
40. TRACTOR
41. BOTTLE
42. D
43. F
44. E
45. A
46. B
47. C
48. CKEABGEF
49. FGEKDBCED
50. ENABLE
51. GAIETY
52. ATTORNEY
53. LANGUAGE
54. TEA
55. Y
56. X
57. W
58. Y
59. LEMONADE
60. TUESDAY
61. 20TH
62. FEBRUARY
63. 28TH
64. THURSDAY
65. U
66. O
67. JP
68. GGP
69. NPO
70. VVK
71. MISER
72. HATCHET
73. ORBIT
74. STUDIO
75. LARDER
76. COMIC
77. £18
78. £18
79. £15
80. £13
81. (2 + 3) - (6 - 4) **
82. (4 + 6 + 3) x2 **
83. (6 + 2) x 4 - 3) **
84. (3 x 4) - (6 - 2) **
85. (3 - 2) + (6 x 4) **

Answers to Test 19

1. E
2. T
3. A
4. 7
5. 7
6. 6
7. 4
8. AND WAS
9. THE AN
10. IN TOO
11. TO COULD
12. BEFORE CHEW
13. LONG HIS
14. 13.8
15. 10.6
16. 21.3
17. 23.2
18. 9.4
19. 23.2
20. L
21. T
22. M
23. R or B
24. G
25. C
26. OUT PUT
27. BAND IT
28. TO WING
29. DEAD LOCK
30. RAN SACK
31. PORT ABLE
32. NICE PEACE
33. BARN NOOSE
34. EAR EARLY
35. MANAGE HARD
36. AUNT BARGE
37. PAT GERM
38. MARATHON SPRINT
39. CHAIR THRONE
40. BARLEY WHEAT
41. ECSTATIC HAPPY
42. PUZZLING DIFFICULT
43. CUT LOP
44. OFF
45. MATCH
46. DARK
47. FAINT
48. LIT
49. HOUSE
50. B
51. C
52. SULBY
53. WIDFORD
54. PICTON
55. 47
56. 2.4
57. 24
58. 25, 51
59. 9, 15
60. 16 (X - 5 + 7)
61. 33 (3 X + 3)
62. 5 (Sq root X - 1)
63. 69 (X cubed + 5)
64. 7 (1/2 X - 5)
65. 15 (cubed root X + 11)
66. GIRL
67. SHARE
68. TRUE
69. WIRE
70. BOAT
71. MAKE
72. 42 (2X + 2)
73. 7 (X ÷ 3) - 3
74. 124 (X cubed - 1)
75. 46 (2 X - 2)
76. 16 (X ÷ 2) +1
77. 82 (X sq + 1)
78. T
79. F
80. T
81. F
82. F
83. ROBOT BEAR
84. LANDED DEAL
85. TAME CHEAT

Answers to Test 20

1. C
2. T
3. N
4. 40
5. £1.80
6. £1.25
7. THAT COMPLAINED
8. THE WAS
9. CAKE TROLLEY
10. THREE THE
11. THE FIND
12. UP FARE
13. 6.3
14. 1.6
15. 3.4
16. 3.9
17. 0.0
18. M
19. T
20. N
21. Y
22. E
23. L
24. AFTER TASTE
25. SEE DING
26. NO VICE
27. FEAT HER
28. HUM AN
29. FLAT TEN
30. HAND BLEED
31. CART HELPED
32. BROOM EDIT
33. PILL BELLOW
34. FLOW BERET
35. NEUTRAL
36. BEWARE
37. SALARY
38. THEATRE
39. PROTECT
40. STRING
41. C
42. D
43. A
44. E
45. B
46. MEDICAL
47. DOUBLE
48. SCARLET
49. LUKEWARM
50. GENERAL
51. ELEPHANT
52. (7+5+4) - 8 **
53. (7-4) + (8-5) **
54. 3 x (4+5+6) **
55. (7x5) - (4x8) **
56. (8-7) - (5-4) **
57. (8+5 - 7) x 4 **
58. A
59. B
60. B
61. C
62. NO
63. YES
64. FRANCE
65. ENGLAND
66. IRELAND
67. ENGLAND
68. FRANCE
69. 9
70. 312
71. 14.10
72. L
73. PNO
74. PFL
75. SPANNER PLIERS
76. GOLF NETBALL
77. TADPOLE CALF
78. BRIDE BOUQUET
79. SILK LEATHER
80. DUBLIN PARIS
81. TSPMWL
82. WIGVIX
83. XEPOMRK
84. ENGINE
85. AUTHOR

** Other answers may be correct.